A Relaxing Country Christmas

Holiday Recipes you Should have got from your Grandmother!

By Carson and Kathy Wyatt

© 2017

Table of Contents

Contents

Introduction 8

Chapter 1: Traditional Christmas Drinks 9

   Butter Grog 9

   Irish Mulled Wine 10

   French Drinking Chocolate 12

   Plain Eggnog 14

   Spiced Eggnog 16

   Hot Buttered Rum 17

   Traditional Wassail 19

   Glogg 21

   Traditional Christmas Punch 23

   Mulled Cider 25

   Fresh Cranberry Punch 28

Chapter 2: Christmas Dinner Recipes 31

   Roasted Duck & Orange Bourbon Molasses Glaze 32

   Grilled Cornish Hens 34

   Coq Au Vin 36

   Parmesan Lamb Shanks 38

   Sweet Curry Glazed Lamb 41

   Cranberry Glazed Ham 42

   Swedish Christmas Ham 44

   Crusted Beef Tenderloin 46

   Sweet Glazed Goose 48

   Tenderloin with a Mustard Cream Sauce 50

   Parmesan Chicken Schnitzels 52

   Coca-Cola Ham 55

Cider Pork Shoulder 56

Beef Wellington 58

Pheasant on a Bed of Wild Rice 61

Brisket & Gravy 63

Sweet Bourbon Glazed Ham 66

Spiced Beef 67

Cherry Pork Loin 69

Crusted Salmon 70

Crusted Rib Roast 72

Chapter 3: Christmas Side Dishes 75

Cream Cheese Mashed Potatoes 75

Simple Roasted Asparagus 76

Smooth Mac & Cheese 76

Creamy Brussel Sprouts 78

Walnut & Citrus Salad 79

Garlic Green Beans 80

Roasted Winter Vegetables 81

Spice Glazed Carrots 81

Braised Cabbage & Bacon 82

Glazed Parsnips & Turnips 83

Potato Gratin 84

Brussel Sprouts & Apples 85

Lively Green Beans 86

Sweet Potato Casserole 88

Baked Onions 89

Classic Butterbeans 90

Homemade Crescent Rolls 91

Cheesy Squash Casserole 92

Spiced Honey Citrus Salad 93

Simple House Rolls 94

Country Corn Casserole 95

Lemon Roasted Cauliflower 96

Roasted Butternut Squash 96

Roasted Chestnuts 98

Old fashioned Collard Green Gratin 99

Nutmeg Popovers 100

Roasted Sweet Potatoes 101

Classic Sausage Stuffing 102

Classic Green Bean Casserole 104

Apples & Cornbread 105

Potato & Leek Gratin 106

Cheddar Biscuits 107

Chapter 4: Traditional Christmas Treats 109

Holiday Fruitcake 109

Traditional Figgy Pudding 111

Classic Panettone 113

Old-Fashioned Authentic German Stollen (Christmas Bread) 116

Salted Caramel Pears 119

Blood Orange Tiramisu 119

Sugared Cranberries 121

Chocolate Pretzels 122

Gingerbread 123

Baked Alaska 126

Fig Holiday Cake Roll 127

Christmas Fruit Tart 129

Old Fashion Divinity 130

Classic Chocolate Fudge 132

Cranberry & Pecan Shortbread 133

Thumbprint Cookies 135

Bread Pudding & Vanilla Sauce 136

Traditional Struffoli 138

Piedmontese Hazelnut Cake 141

Classic Christmas Pudding 143

Southern Pecan Pie 146

Chapter 5: Christmas Jarred Gift Recipes 150

Jarred Spiced Butter & Fresh Pound Cake... 151

Jarred Peppermint Brownies 152

Mocha Cocoa 152

Rosemary & Mint Sugar Scrub 153

Jasmine Bath Salts 154

Jarred Cranberry Cookie Mix 154

Cinnamon Popcorn 155

Jarred Tropical Tea Soak... 155

Jarred Apple Butter... 156

Spiced Pear Jam 157

Cranberry Honey Butter 158

Spiced Gingerbread Jelly 158

Poultry Dry Rub... 159

Cranberry & Pumpkin Bread 160

Spiced Gingerbread Syrup... 160

Jarred Cinnamon Pancakes 161

Blondie Toffee Bars... 162

Ranch Dip Mix.. 163

Banana Pudding Snack Mix 163

French Vanilla Cocoa Mix.. 164

Conclusion... 165

Introduction

So you want to have a country Christmas. No one can blame you for wanting to take Christmas back to good old fashion country roots with authentic recipes and traditional goodies. You'll find everything you need to start your own family traditions or revive old ones long lost in this book! You'll find Christmas drink, including a spiced eggnog, dessert recipes such as divinity and fruitcake, and dinner recipes that will certainly blow your family away. With recipes like Swedish Christmas ham, it'll be hard to choose what to cook for dinner. There's no reason to deal with 'modern' when you can have a classic Christmas for you and your family. It has helped us and our family to have one of the most joyous Christmas holiday seasons every year.

Sincerely,

Carson and Kathy Wyatt

Chapter 1: Traditional Christmas Drinks

Sometimes it can be just as hard to figure out what drinks to serve to your family and friends as it is to figure out what to feed them. Eggnog is a traditional choice, you'll certainly find it in the list, but there are so many authentic Christmas drinks to choose from. Some of them long forgotten by many, but still just as sure to delight your taste buds now as they did way back then.

Butter Grog

This buttery mulled cider is popular around Christmas, and you'll find that many people in Germany especially seem to enjoy the drink. To make it alcoholic, just add three to four ounces of your favorite rum, or a little more if you like, instead of using the rum extract.

Yields: 4-6

Time: 45 Minutes

Ingredients:

- 1 ½ Tablespoon Butter
- 1 Tablespoon Dark Brown Sugar
- 4 Cup Apple Cider, Fresh is Best
- 2 Cinnamon Sticks
- 4 Cloves, Whole
- Zest of 1 Lemon
- 1 Medium Orange, Juiced with Zest reserved
- 2 Teaspoons Rum Extract
- 1 Inch Piece Ginger Root, Sliced & Peeled

Directions:

1. Start by melting your butter in a saucepan over medium heat. You'll then want to add your cloves, cinnamon, brown sugar, cider, and lemon and orange zest.
2. Add in your ginger and orange juice, and mix well.
3. Let your liquid start to simmer before removing the pan from heat.

4. Add in your rum extract, stirring well.
5. Let it stand for thirty minutes to steep, and then strain.
6. Reheat it and make sure to serve warm.

Irish Mulled Wine

For an adult Christmas part this is perfect! You'll find it originates from Ireland, and it's perfect for a party.

Yields: 12-15 Cups

Time: 2+ Hours

Ingredients:

- 6 Ounces Dark Brown Sugar
- 2 Sticks Cinnamon
- 3 Star Anise
- 1 Bottle Red Wine, Dry
- ½ Bottle Ruby Port
- 4 Dozen Cloves (give or take to taste)
- 1 Orange, Large
- 1 Lemon, Unwaxed

Directions:

1. Start by paring your orange and lemon, removing the pith.
2. Stud the fruit with cloves all over. Add these to a large saucepan and a pint of water.
3. Turn your heat to medium, and add cinnamon, star anise, and brown sugar, mixing well. Some people will add the orange and lemon peel at this point if they choose to use it.
4. Stir over heat, making sure that the sugar is dissolved.
5. Let it simmer for an hour. It will be stronger if you let it sit for a day after this hour.
6. Strain, discarding your fruit and spices, and then return it to your pan.
7. Add your port and red wine, reheating it to a boil.
8. Serve hot, and you can garnish with lemon slices and orange slices. Some people even like a dash of nutmeg.

Irish Mulled Wine

French Drinking Chocolate

This decadent chocolate drink is more than your average hot chocolate, and it's a perfect Christmas drink for kids or adults. It's a thick drink with a silky texture that's sure to delight both family and friends.

Yields: 4-6

Time: 25 Minutes

Ingredients:

- 8 Ounces Chocolate Bars, Bittersweet
- 1 ¾ Cup Whole Milk
- ¾ Teaspoon Vanilla Extract, Pure
- 2 Tablespoons Light Brown Sugar
- ½ Cup Heavy Cream

Directions:

1. Start by breaking your chocolate into small pieces, and then placing them in a sauce pot.
2. Turn the heat onto medium-low, adding your cream, vanilla extract, milk and brown sugar, stirring well.
3. Make sure to continue stirring until it comes to a low simmer and your chocolate is completely melted. You should not stop until it's slightly thickened and completely smooth. It is much thicker than hot chocolate. However, make sure that it isn't as thick as chocolate fondue.
   If you need to, add another ¼ cup whole milk, and then stir until it comes back to a simmer again.
4. Drink warm.

Plain Eggnog

This is a traditional plain eggnog recipe that can be spiked if desired. Do not mistake it for spiced eggnog.

Yields: 6-7

Time: 30 Minutes

Ingredients:

- 4 Egg Yolks
- 1 Pint Whole Milk
- 4 Egg Whites
- 1/3 Cup Cane Sugar
- 1 Tablespoon Cane Sugar
- 3 Ounces Bourbon (Optional)
- 1 Teaspoon Nutmeg, Grated
- 1 Cup Heavy Cream

Directions:

1. Start by beating your egg yolks until their color lightens.
2. Add in your third of a cup of sugar gradually, continuing to beat until the sugar is dissolved completely.
3. Once dissolved, slowly add in your milk, cream, bourbon and nutmeg. Stir until it's well combined.
4. Place your egg whites in a bowl, and beat to soft peaks.
5. Add in your tablespoon of sugar while running, and continue to beat until stiff peaks start to form.
6. Whisk in your egg whites into your egg yolk mixture.
7. Chill before serving.

Egg Nog

Spiced Eggnog

This spiced eggnog recipe is southern, and you'll find it has that southern Christmas comfort too.

Yields: 3-4 Cups

Time: 2 Hours 30 Minutes

Ingredients:

- 4 Egg Yolks
- 4 Egg Whites
- ½ Cup Cane Sugar
- 2 Cups Whole Milk
- 2-4 Cloves, Whole
- 1 Stick Cinnamon
- 1 Cup Heavy Cream
- 1 Teaspoon Nutmeg, Grated
- 1 Teaspoon Vanilla Extract, Pure
- 2 Tablespoons Bourbon (Optional)

Directions:

1. Start by beating your egg yolks in a large bowl. They should become thick and pale, and then gradually beat in your sugar until it's blended well.
2. Stir in your milk, cloves and cinnamon.
3. Cook over medium heat, stirring constantly. It should take eight to ten minutes to bring to a boil around the edges. Do not let it come to a boil.
4. Gradually stir in half of your hot milk mixture into your egg mixture.
5. Stir in your remaining egg mixture, stirring well.
6. Cook over medium heat for seven to eight minutes while stirring continuously. It should thicken and begin to coat the back of your spoon. Do not boil. It should reach 160 degrees.
7. Remove from heat, stirring in your cream and then staring.
8. Let cool for an hour before mixing in your vanilla, nutmeg and bourbon.
9. Let chill for an hour more before serving.

Hot Buttered Rum

This is an all adult drink that's popular in Europe and some parts of the US. It's a great way to start the holiday season and warm you up!

Serves: 8

Time: 1 Hour 25 Minutes

Ingredients:

- 2 Quarts Hot Water
- 3-4 Cinnamon Sticks
- ½ Cup Butter (Not Margarine)
- ½-1 Teaspoon Nutmeg, Grated
- 6-8 Whole Cloves

- 1 Cup Whipped Cream, Sweetened
- 2 Cups Dark Brown Sugar
- 2 Cups Rum
- ¼ Teaspoon Sea Salt, Fine

Directions:

1. Start by combining your hot water, salt, butter, and brown sugar in a medium saucepan. Bring to a simmer before adding cinnamon and cloves. Remember to keep it over medium heat the entire time.
2. Reduce to a low simmer and let sit for one hour, stirring in your rum once done.
3. Ladle into mugs and serve with whipped cream and a small dash of nutmeg.

Traditional Wassail

Wassail is a traditional Christmas drink from England. It was traditionally served on the twelfth night of celebration or Christmas Eve. It was a part of wassailing, which was to go from house to house singing Christmas carols.

Yields: 1 Pitcher

Time: 1 Hour 5 Minutes

Ingredients:

- 4 Small Apples
- 1 Medium Orange
- 13-15 Whole Cloves
- ¼ Cup Cane Sugar, Unrefined
- 2 Quarts Hard Apple Cider
- 1 Tablespoon Ginger, Powdered
- 1 Teaspoon Nutmeg, Grated
- 6 Allspice Berries
- 2 Cinnamon Sticks
- 6 Large Eggs, Separated
- ½-¾ Cup Brandy

Directions:

1. Start by heating your oven to 350.
2. Scoop the core of your apples out, but try not to fully penetrate the. It's best to use a melon baller.
3. Fill your apples with your cane sugar, placing them on a baking sheet.
4. Stud an orange with thirteen cloves, placing it on your baking sheet as well.
5. Bake your apples and orange for forty minutes.
6. While this is baking, pour your apple cider and brandy into a stock pot with a heavy bottom. Warm it over medium-low heat.
7. Whisk in your powdered ginger and nutmeg, but do not bring it to a boil.
8. Cut a square of butter muslin, placing your cinnamon and allspice into it. Tie it with cooking twine, and let this sachet float in your wassail as it warms.
9. Beat your egg yolks until they turn light in color in a separate bowl, setting this aside.
10. Take another bowl and whip your egg whites until they form stiff peaks.
11. Fold your egg yolks into your egg whites.
12. You'll now need to temper the eggs by pouring one half of a cup of your wassail into your eggs.
13. Remove your spice sachet from the wassail, and finish pouring your wassail into your tempered eggs.
14. Transfer to a punch bowl.
15. Float your apples and orange into the wassail. Let sit for about thirty minutes before serving.

Glogg

This is an authentic drink recipe that's traditional in Scandinavian countries. It's similar to mulled wine as well as wassail, but it has some unique twists such as the cardamom pods, and the raisins and almonds are commonly used for garnish.

Serves: 10

Time: 25 Minutes

Ingredients:

- 4 Cups Water
- 1 Cup Brandy (Or Spiced Rum)
- Peel of 1 Large Orange, Cut into Strips
- 2 Tablespoons Whole Cloves
- 2 Teaspoons Vanilla Extract, Pure
- 10 Cardamom Pods
- ½ Inch ginger, Peeled & Crushed
- ½ Teaspoon Nutmeg, Grated Fresh
- 4 Sticks Cinnamon
- 750 ml Red Wine, Dry
- 1 Cup Vodka
- 2/3 Cup Dark Brown Sugar

Directions:

1. Heat your brandy, spices and water, bringing it to a boil.
2. Reduce the heat and allow it to simmer for ten to fifteen minutes.

3. Add in your vodka, wine and sugar, mixing well. Let simmer while stirring until your sugar is dissolved.
4. Strain out your orange peel and cloves. Leave all of your other spices behind.

Top with raisins and almonds, serving warm.

CHRISTMAS IN FINLAND

Traditional Christmas Punch

If Wassail is a little too old school, you may still like this holiday Christmas punch. It's been around for ages, and it has a slightly less heavy taste due to the tea that's been added.

Serves: 25

Time: 20 Minutes

Ingredients:

- 1 Bottle (750 mls) Dark Rum
- 2 Bottles (750 mls each) Red Wine, Dry
- 3 Cups Black Tea, Unsweetened
- ½ Cup Orange Juice
- ½ Cup Lemon Juice
- 2 Cups Cane Sugar

Directions:

1. Start by combining your juices, tea and wine into a large saucepan over medium heat. Heat well, making sure it comes to a simmer.
2. Stir in your sugar gradually, and then gradually mix in your rum.
3. Serve warm.

Christmas at our Ranch

Mulled Cider

Cider is a traditional drink for Christmas or just the cold winter months, and it's sure to be a delight at any party or gathering!

Yields: 1 Gallon

Time: 30 Minutes

Ingredients:

- 10 Whole Cloves
- ½ Teaspoon Whole Black Peppercorns, Crushed Lightly
- 2 Strips Orange Peel, 2 Inches Long Each
- 6 Allspice Berries, Dried
- 4 Heads Star Anise
- 1 cinnamon Stick
- 1 Inch Piece Ginger, Peeled & Sliced Thin
- 1 Gallon Apple Juice, Unfiltered

Directions:

1. Combine all ingredients in a pot, and then bring it to a boil over medium-high heat. Reduce it to a simmer, simmering for ten minutes.
2. Remove from heat, letting it steep for another ten minutes before serving warm.

Old Time Tree Decorating Tip!

Thread strands of popcorn and fresh cranberries with needle and thread and put around your Christmas tree. This is a very old fashioned practice that you can magically relive this Christmas!

Fresh Cranberry Punch

This Christmas punch brings another traditional flavor to the table, and it's easy to make. You can use thawed or fresh cranberries, but many people find frozen ones to be a little easier to find.

Serves: 12

Time: 30 Minutes

Ingredients:

- 4 Cups Cranberries
- 3 ½ Quarters Water
- 4 Cinnamon Sticks
- ¾ Cup Orange Juice
- 2/3 Cup Lemon Juice
- 12 Whole Cloves
- 2 Cups Cane Sugar

Directions:

1. Combine your cranberries, water, cinnamon and cloves in a large stock pot. Bring it to a boil before covering.
2. Reduce heat, simmering for twelve to fifteen minutes.
3. Strain, and then add in your lemon juice and orange juice.
4. Stir well before gradually adding your sugar, stirring until dissolved. Serve hot.

Chapter 2: Christmas Dinner Recipes

It doesn't matter if you're hosting a Christmas dinner party, going to a pot luck or just cooking for family. You'll find various traditional Christmas recipes from around the world in this section that are sure to delight your taste buds and all those you serve it to! Country cooking prides itself on tradition and taste, and none of these recipes are lacking.

Roasted Duck & Orange Bourbon Molasses Glaze

Duck is a traditional Christmas dinner in many parts of the world, especially in Europe. It's a tradition that carried into the states and when paired with an orange bourbon molasses glaze it's the perfect mix of savory and sweet to put on your table.

Serves: 8-10

Time: 11 Hours 50 Minutes

Ingredients:

- 2 Whole Ducks (6-7 lbs Each)
- 2 Teaspoons Sea Salt, Fine
- ½ Teaspoon Black Pepper, Ground
- 1 Cup Orange Marmalade
- ¼ Teaspoon Ginger, Ground
- ¼ Teaspoon Crushed Red Pepper
- 1 Tablespoon Lemon Juice, Fresh

- 3 Tablespoons Molasses, Raw
- ¼ Cup Bourbon

Directions:

1. Start by removing your giblets from the duck, and then reserve them for some other use. Many people use them in stuffing.
2. Rinse your ducks, and then pat them dry. Remove any excess skin and fat.
3. Tie the legs together, and then chill without it being covered for ten to twenty-four hours.
4. Start by heating you oven to 40.
5. You should let your duck stand for fifteen minutes at room temperature before pricking the thighs, breast and legs with a fork.
6. Rub your duck with black pepper and salt, placing it breast side up on your pan. It should be lined with aluminum foil, and bake for forty-five minutes.
7. Stir your orange marmalade, molasses, lemon juice, crushed red pepper, ginger and bourbon together in a saucepan, bringing it to a boil over high heat.
8. Reduce the heat to a medium-low and continue to cook for ten to fifteen minutes. Stir often, continuing to cook until it's reduced to about a cup.
9. Remove your ducks from the oven, and spoon the fat from your pan.
10. Brush the ducks down with your glaze, and reduce your oven temperature to 350.
11. Bake for twenty to twenty-five minutes. The meat thermometer should be inserted into your thickest portion and register 180 when it's done.
12. Let it stand for at least fifteen minutes before serving.

Grilled Cornish Hens

Cornish hens are a great way to personalize Christmas dinner for all of your guests, but it doesn't have to be hard. Grilling can be an easy and fun way to prepare dinner, especially in winter months.

Serves: 6

Time: 11 Hours

Ingredients:

- 2 Tablespoons Flat Leaf Parsley Leaves, Fresh
- 6 Cornish Hens, 20 Ounces Each
- 2 Tablespoons Thyme Leaves, Fresh
- ½ Teaspoon Onion Powder
- ½ Teaspoon Garlic Powder
- 1 ½ Teaspoons Ground Black Pepper
- 3 Tablespoons Sea Salt, Fine

Directions:

1. Start by processing your salt, black pepper, onion powder, garlic powder, thyme leaves and parsley together in a food processor until well combined. It should take about twenty seconds.
2. Pat it down with your herb mixture.
3. Pat your hens dry, and then place them with the breast side down on a cutting board.
4. Cut your hens using your kitchen shears along the backbone. Discard the bone, and then turn them breast side up. Press against the breastbone until you hear the bone crack. Tuck your wings under, and then place them on a parchment paper pan.
5. Sprinkle the salt mixture over your hens, chilling uncovered for ten to twenty-four hours.
6. Start by heating your grill to medium-high heat, and then grill them with the side down for eight minutes on each side. You'll want your girl lid covering them, and when you insert a meat thermometer at the thickest portion it should register 165. Let stand for five minutes before serving.

Coq Au Vin

This is a variation from a French dish that uses wine braised chicken. However white wine is used instead of red, which results in a golden hue. It's still a modern take on a traditional Christmas classic.

Serves: 6

Time: 3 Hours 20 Minutes

Ingredients:

- ½ Teaspoon Black Pepper
- ½ Teaspoon Sea Salt
- 6 Chicken Leg Quarters, 4-5 lbs
- 2 Tablespoons Extra Virgin Olive Oil
- 12 Ounces Bacon at ½ Inch Thickness

- 16 Ounces Cremini Mushrooms, Chopped
- 2-3 Celery Ribs, Chopped
- 1 Yellow Onion, Chopped
- 6 Ounces Tomato Paste
- 3 Cups White Wine, Dry
- 32 Ounces Chicken Broth, Reduced Sodium
- 2 Rosemary Sprigs, Fresh
- 6 Thyme Sprigs, Fresh
- 6 Ounces Baby Carrots
- 1 Tablespoon Butter

Directions:

1. Start by heating your oven to 350.
2. Sprinkle your salt and pepper into the chicken, and cook your leg quarters over medium-high heat until each side is browned and cooked through.
3. Cook your bacon next, removing once crisp. Drain on paper towels.
4. Sauté your mushrooms, celery ribs and onion together over medium-high heat for six minutes or until golden brown. Stir in your garlic, sautéing for another minute.
5. Next, stir in your tomato paste as well as a cup of wine, cooking over medium-high heat and stirring often for about two minutes.
6. Add the remaining two cups of wine, and bring it to a boil. Stir occasionally, and continue until it's reduced by half.
7. Add the bacon and chicken to your mushroom mixture. Place in a Dutch oven and add your broth, thyme, rosemary, and baby carrots. Cover with a tight fitting lid.
8. Bake for one and a half hours to 350. The meat should start to pull away from the bone.
9. Put your oven rack seven inches from heat when it's turned on the broiler.
10. Reserve your cooking liquid and vegetables. Place your chicken on the greased wire rack.
11. Broil your chicken for two minutes, which should turn it a golden brown and crisp the skin.
12. Transfer to a serving platter. Skim the fat from your liquid and discard your herbs.
13. Bring the liquid to a simmer over medium-high heat, and stir occasionally.

14.   Remove it from heat, and add your butter, whisking until it forms a smooth sauce. Serve this with your chicken.

Parmesan Lamb Shanks

Lamb is yet another common Christmas dish, and it's perfect to impress your family.

Serves: 6

Time: 5 Hours

Ingredients:

- 6 Lamb Shanks
- 2 Tablespoons Tomato Paste
- ¼ Cup Extra Virgin Olive Oil
- 1 Cup Red Wine
- 10 ½ Ounces Beef Consommé, Canned
- 6 Flat Leaf Parsley Sprigs

- 4-6 Bay Leaves
- 4 Thyme Sprigs, Fresh
- 2 Celery Ribs, Chopped in 1 Inch Pieces
- 3 Orange Peel Strips, 1 Inch Pieces
- 1 Large Carrot, Cut into 1 Inch Pieces
- 1 Onion, Cut into Wedges
- 1-2 Rosemary Sprigs, Fresh
- 4 Tablespoons Butter, Divided
- 1 ½ Cups Panko
- 1 Cup Parmigiano-Reggiano, Finely Grated (or Parmesan of your choice)
- 2 ½ Teaspoons Thyme, Freshly Chopped
- 1 Teaspoon Rosemary, Freshly Chopped

Directions:

1. Start by heating the oven to 325.
2. Season your lamb with your pepper and salt, letting stand for thirty minutes at room temperature.
3. Cook your lamb shanks over medium-high heat for two minutes. Make sure it's cooked all the way through.
4. Next, cook your tomato paste in your lamb shank drippings. It'll take about thirty seconds for your tomato paste to char slightly, and then add in your wine. Bring the mixture to a boil, and boil for three minutes. Your mixture should reduce to about one third of a cup.
5. Stir in your consommé, parsley, thyme, bay leaves, orange peel, celery ribs, carrot and onion together.
6. Add a cup of water and add your lamb back in.
7. Place in an oven safe pan, and then bake at 325 for three hours. The meat should be tender and pull away from the bone.
8. Let it stand for thirty minutes at room temperature.
9. Melt your butter in a skillet, adding your pan and cook over medium0high heat for a minute or until lightly browned. Make sure that you stir often.
10. Toss your panko mixture with your thyme, rosemary, and cheese. Place in a small bowl.
11. Preheat your broiler with your oven rack seven inches from heat.
12. Remove your shanks from the pan, reserving the cooking liquid.
13. Dredge your shanks in your panko mixture making sure it's pressed to the surface.

14. Spray them lightly with cooking spray and put them on a lightly greased rack in a broiler pan. Broil for about two to three minutes on each side. It should be golden and crisp.
15. Skim the fat from your cooking liquid, pouring through a strainer and into a saucepan. Discard all of the solids, bringing the drippings to simmer over medium-high heat.
16. Let this mixture simmer for about five minutes, making sure to whisk occasionally. It should reduce, and then remove from heat.
17. Add in your remaining butter, whisking until it melts and is smooth. Serve this sauce over your lamb.

Sweet Curry Glazed Lamb

Since lamb is traditionally served on Christmas by many, here's another sweet lamb recipe that is often served with roasted cranberries and grapes.

Serves: 6

Time: 1 Hour 10 Minutes

Ingredients:

- 1 Tablespoon Red Curry Powder
- 1 ½ Teaspoons Ground Pepper
- 1 ½ Teaspoons Sea Salt
- 5 Tablespoons Extra Virgin Olive Oil
- 2 Tablespoons Honey, Raw
- 2 Lamb Rib Roasts (8 Ribs, about 2 ½ lbs Each), Trimmed

Directions:

1. Start by heating your oven to 425.
2. Sprinkle your lamb with curry powder, pepper and salt, letting stand for thirty minutes.
3. Cook your lamb in hot oil. It's best to use a twelve inch cast-iron skillet. Cook for six to seven minutes over medium heat, and turn often. This should brown the sides and tops.
4. Place your lamb with the meat side up in your skillet.
5. Stir in your remaining four tablespoons of extra virgin olive oil and honey, brushing the lamb with the mixture.
6. Bake for fifteen to eighteen minutes at 425. When inserting your meat thermometer into your thickest portion it should be 130.
7. Remove it from the oven, letting stand for ten minutes before cutting it into chops and serving.

Cranberry Glazed Ham

Ham is a traditional Christmas dish, and this cranberry glaze gives a traditional and holiday taste to the dish.

Serves: 15

Time: 1 Hour 40 minutes

Ingredients:

- 14 Ounces Cranberry Sauce, Whole Berry
- 4 lb Boneless Ham, Fully Cooked
- ½ Cup Maple Syrup

- ¼ Cup Apple Cider Vinegar
- 1 ½ Teaspoons Ground Mustard

Directions:

1. Start by heating your oven to 325, and then line a roasting pan with foil. Place your ham in your pan, baking for an hour covered.
2. In a small saucepan, whisk all of your other ingredients together making sure they're well blended. Remove a cup of the mixture for glaze. The remaining mixture will be used for sauce.
3. Brush your ham with your glaze mix, and then bake for thirty-five to forty-five minutes. Brush every ten minutes with the remaining glaze.
4. Warm your sauce mixture over medium heat, and stir occasionally. Serve this with your ham.

Swedish Christmas Ham

If you've ever had that Christmas ham you just couldn't repeat but it seemed traditional and sweet, it was probably a version of the Swedish Christmas ham. Here's a traditional recipe that will knock the socks off of all of your guests.

Serves: 6-8

Time: 5 Hours 35 Minutes

Ingredients:

- 7-9 lbs Salt Cured Ham, Unsmoked
- 1 Tablespoon Dark Brown Sugar
- 2 Large Egg Yolks
- 6 Tablespoons Gingersnaps, Finely Crumbled
- 6 Tablespoons Swedish Mustard

Directions:

1. Start by turning your oven to 350. The oven rack should be placed in the upper third of your oven, and then you'll want to rinse your ham to help remove any excess salt. Make sure to pat it dry gently.
2. The rind side should be placed up in a heavy roasting pan, and then put your pan in the oven. Roast your ham for about four and a half hours. Remove it from your oven.
3. Now, turn the oven up to 450.
4. Slice the rind off of your ham, and then whisk your egg yolks, mustard and brown sugar together. Spread this over the entire surface of your ham as evenly as possible.
5. Sprinkle your crumbled gingersnaps over it, and then cook in your oven for an additional fifteen minutes. It should turn a golden brown.
6. Remove from heat, and then let rest while covered for fifteen minutes. Carve and serve it warm.

Crusted Beef Tenderloin

Beef tenderloin is another meat that's commonly served around the holidays, and with a crusted texture it's delicious and looks wonderful when plating.

Serves: 6-8

Time: 2 Hours 20 Minutes

Ingredients:

- 4-5lb Beef Tenderloin, Trimmed
- 3 Teaspoons Sea Salt, Divided
- 3-4 Cloves Garlic, Pressed
- ¾ Cup Panko
- 2 Teaspoons Ground Pepper, Divided

- 3 Tablespoons Olive Oil, Divided
- 1 ¼ Cup Potato Chips, Kettle Cooked & Crushed
- ¼ Cup Parsley, Chopped Fine
- 1-2 Bay Leaves, Crushed
- 1 Tablespoon Thyme, Freshly Chopped
- 1 Tablespoon Dijon Mustard
- 1 Egg White, Lightly Beaten
- Sage for Garnish

Directions:

1. Start by heating your oven to 400.
2. Prepare your tenderloin by sprinkling it with two teaspoon of sea salt, and then let it stand for about forty minutes.
3. Sauté your panko, garlic, one teaspoon of pepper, and remaining teaspoon of sea salt in a tablespoon of oil. Use a skillet over medium heat. Cook for two to three minutes, and it should turn a golden brown.
4. Let it cool completely, which will take about ten minutes.
5. Stir in your potato chips, parsley, thyme, bay leaves and egg whites.
6. Pat your tenderloin dry using a paper towel, and then sprinkle with the remaining pepper.
7. Brown your beef in two tablespoons of your oil using a roasting pan over medium-high heat. It should be browned on all sides, which takes about two to three minutes on each side.
8. Transfer to a wire rack on a lined pan, and then let stand for ten minutes.
9. Spread the mustard over your tenderloin, and then press your panko mixture on the top and sides of your tenderloin.
10. Bake at 400 for about forty to forty-five minutes. The coating should become crisp. It should be rare, and then let stand for ten minutes before serving.

Sweet Glazed Goose

Goose is another commonly served meat for Christmas, but now you usually have to make a trip to a local butcher shop or farm to get it. Still, it'll be worth the extra work with this relatively easy and tasty dish.

Serves: 8-10

Time: 3 Hours 5 Minutes

Ingredients:

- 2 Garlic Cloves, Minced

- ¾ Cup Orange Marmalade
- 1 Teaspoon Sea Salt, Fine
- 10-12 lb Goose
- 2 Navel Oranges, Small & Quartered
- 3 Tablespoons Dijon Mustard
- 1 Tablespoon Light Brown Sugar
- ½ Teaspoon Black Pepper
- 2 Tablespoons Soy Sauce, Reduced Sodium
- 1 Small Onion, Quartered

Directions:

1. Start by sprinkling the inside of the cavity with salt, and then prick the skin with a fork.
2. Place your garlic, onion and oranges in the cavity.
3. Tuck the wings of your goose under, and then it the drumsticks together, placing it on the rack in a roasting pan with the breast facing up.
4. Turn the oven to 350, and then bake uncovered for 2 hours and forty-five minutes to three hours fifteen minutes. You'll want to cover loosely with foil if you feel your goose is browning too quickly. Depending on your goose, you may need to drain the fat from the pan as well.
5. Get out a saucepan, and then combine your soy sauce, brown sugar, pepper, mustard and marmalade together.
6. Stir over medium heat, cooking until heated through. Before your goose is done, usually in the last fifteen minutes, you'll want to baste this glaze over your goose.
7. Let stand for fifteen minutes before serving.

Tenderloin with a Mustard Cream Sauce

This is one main dish that is easy to make, and the sauce is too! Don't let the long ingredient list scare you away because it'll be well worth the extra prep time.

Serves: 10-12

Time: 2 Hours 10 Minutes

Ingredients:

- 2 ½ Teaspoons Sea Salt
- 1 Teaspoon Black Pepper
- ½ Teaspoon Ground Cumin
- 1 Teaspoon Garlic Powder
- 1 Teaspoon Thyme, Dried
- ½ Teaspoon Red Pepper, Ground
- ½ Teaspoon Paprika

- 5-6 lb Beef Tenderloin, Trimmed
- 1 Tablespoon Olive Oil
- Vegetable Cooking Spray

Sauce:

- 1 Shallot, Minced
- 1 Tablespoon Olive Oil
- 1 Cup White Wine, Dry
- 1-2 Garlic Cloves, Minced
- ¼ Cup Creole Mustard
- 2 Teaspoons White Sugar
- 8 Ounces Sour Cream
- 1 Teaspoon Sea Salt
- ¼ Teaspoon Black Pepper, Ground Fresh

Directions:

1. Start by making your sauce to put up. Sauté your shallot over medium heat in a skillet. It'll take about two minutes until soft, and then add your garlic sautéing for another minute.
2. Stir in your wine, sugar, and mustard, brining the mixture to a boil while stirring constantly. Cook at a boil for three minutes, continuing to stir. The mixture should reduce by half and thicken.
3. Start by heating your oven to 500, and then stir in your salt, pepper, garlic, thyme, cumin, paprika and red pepper. Sprinkle this mix over your tenderloin, pressing gently.
4. Cover your tenderloin and let it stand for thirty minutes at room temperature before putting it in a lightly greased roasting pan.
5. Bake for fifteen minutes, and then reduce your oven to 37. Bake for another twenty-five to thirty minutes.
6. Remove from the oven and let stand for ten minutes before slicing.
7. Re-heat your shallot mixture from. Once heated remove from heat, whisking in your pepper, salt and sour cream. Serve on top of your tenderloin.

Parmesan Chicken Schnitzels

If you're looking for a traditional German recipe to put on your Christmas dinner, then you've found the right one!

Serves: 4

Time: 35 Minutes

Ingredients:

- 4 Chicken Breasts, Boneless & Skinless. Pork or Veal cutlets can also be substituted, if desired.
- 4 Tablespoons Bread Crumbs
- 4 Tablespoons Parmesan Cheese, Grated
- 2 Teaspoons Garlic Powder
- 2 Teaspoons Oregano, Dried
- Sea Salt & Black Pepper to Taste

Directions:

1. Start by beating your chicken breasts with a mallet, continuing to beat them until they are flat. You can do this between cling films which will help to cut down on the mess.
2. Mix all of your other ingredients in a large bowl together, and then dip the schnitzels into it before placing them on a non-stick baking pan.
3. Bake at 400 for twenty to twenty-five minutes. The chicken should be cooked through and the coating should be golden and crisp.
4. Serve immediately with lemon wedges.

Christmas in Germany

Coca-Cola Ham

This is an American favorite, and everyone knows that no matter if you call it pop or soda, you've likely had coke if you're an American. Though, most people seem to have forgotten that it is more than a delicious drink. It can make a fabulous tasting ham too!

Serves: 4

Time: 3 Hours

Ingredients:

- 4-5 lb Ham
- 2 Liters Coca-Cola
- 1 Large Onion, Peeled & Halved
- 1 Tablespoon Molasses
- 2 Teaspoons Mustard Powder
- 12-15 Whole Cloves
- 2 Tablespoons Dark Brown Sugar

Directions:

1. Put your ham in a pan, and add in your onions before pouring your coke over it.
2. Bring this to a boil and then reduce it to a simmer, putting a lid on it and cooking for two and a half hours.
3. Start by heating your oven to 450.
4. Pay attention to your ham in your pan, and once it's cooked take it out to cool before removing the skin. Leave a thin layer of fat on it, and then cut diamond shapes into the fat, placing a clove in each one.
5. Pat your mustard and sugar into the sticky fat, and then bake in a pan lined with foil for ten to fifteen minutes. It should become crisp and bubbly.

Cider Pork Shoulder

Pork shoulder is another wonderful main dish to serve on Christmas, and it's spiced up to a seasonal meal with a cider touch.

Serves: 6-8

Time: 13 Hours 15 Minutes

Ingredients:

- 2 Teaspoons Paprika
- 2 Teaspoon Dark Brown Sugar
- 1 Teaspoon Dry Mustard
- 2 Tablespoons Sea Salt
- 4-5 lbs Boneless Pork Shoulder, Butterflied
- 2 Tablespoons Extra Virgin Olive Oil
- 1 Cup Apple Cider
- 3 Cups Chicken Broth, Reduced Sodium
- 1 Tablespoon Honey, Raw
- 2 Tablespoons Dijon Mustard
- 2 Granny Smith Apples
- 6-7 Bay Leaves
- 1 Medium Yellow Onion, Chopped
- 2-3 Garlic Cloves, Minced
- 1 Tablespoon Butter
- 1 Teaspoon Apple Cider Vinegar

Directions:

1. Rub your pork shoulder with your sea salt, brown sugar, paprika, red pepper and dry mustard. Chill for about eight to twelve hours in your fridge uncovered.
2. Heat your oven to 325, and let it stand for about twenty minutes at room temperature.
3. Cook your pork over medium-high heat in a large Dutch oven for about twelve minutes. Brown it on all sides, and then broil your olive oil and chicken broth together over medium-high heat as well. Reduce heat, and then whisk in your mustard. Let it simmer and stir for five minutes occasionally.
4. Return your pork to the oven, and then add in your bay leaves.

5. Slice your apple into thick slices, and then place your garlic, onion and apple slices around your pork.
6. Simmer it over medium heat, and then cover and put it in your Dutch oven again.
7. Bake at 325 for three and a half to four hours. Let your pork stand at room temperature for thirty minutes.
8. Transfer pork onto a serving platter, skimming the fat from your cooking liquid. Strain your liquid, discarding your solids.
9. Simmer the remaining liquid over medium—high heat, and cut your apple into thin slices adding them into your mixture. Let it simmer and stir occasionally until your sauce reduces some. It should take about five minutes. Remove it from heat.
10. Add in your butter and vinegar, and stir until smooth.
11. Serve this sauce with your pork.

Beef Wellington

This is an old American favorite for many people on Christmas or even on New Year's Eve, so why not bring it to your table. It takes a little bit of care, but it'll impress even your hardest guest!

Serves: 4-6

Time: 2 Hours 30 Minutes

Ingredients:

- 3 lbs Fillet of Beef
- 1 cup Chestnut Mushrooms
- 3 Tablespoons Extra Virgin Olive Oil
- 3 ½ Ounces White Wine, Dry
- 3 ½ Tablespoons Butter
- 1 Large Sprig Thyme
- 12 Slices Bacon

- Handful Flour to Dust
- 1 lb Puff Pastry, Thawed
- 2 Egg Yolks, Beaten with 1 Teaspoon Water

Directions:

1. Heat your oven to 400, placing your beef on a roasting tray. Brush with a tablespoon of your olive oil and then season with pepper. Roast for about fifteen minutes if you're looking for medium rare. It'll take about twenty if you want it to be medium. When the beef is cooked, let it cool and then chill in the fridge for twenty minutes.

2. While it's cooling you'll need to chop your mushrooms as fine as you can. Their texture should resemble coarse breadcrumbs, and you can use a food processor for this as well.

3. Heat two tablespoons of oil and all of your butter in a pan to fry your mushrooms over medium heat. Add in your thyme sprig, and cook for about ten minutes while stirring often. Your mixture should soften.

4. Season your mushroom mix and then pour over the wine and cook for roughly ten minutes. The wine should be absorbed, and the mixture should hold its shape when stirred.

5. Remove this mix from the pan, letting it cool. Discard the thyme.

6. Take out a large chopping board and overlap two piece soft plastic wrap over it. Lay your bacon out on the plastic wrap, and then spread half of your mushroom mix over it. Sit the fillet on top, and spread the remaining mushroom mix over it. Use your plastic wrap to draw the bacon around the fillet, and then roll it into a sausage shape, twisting the ends so that it tights as you go. Chill the fillet while you work on rolling out your pastry.

7. Roll a third of your pastry to form a 7x12 strip, placing it on a baking sheet. Roll out your remaining pastry to form an 11x14 inch strip.

8. Unravel your fillet from the plastic, placing it in the center of your smaller strip and then brush the edges with your beaten egg yolk. Use a rolling pin and lift and drape the larger piece over your fillet, pressing the sides down. You'll want to trim the edges to about one and a half inches, sealing it with a fork. Glaze the seal with more egg yolk, and then take a knife to mark the beef wellington with long diagonal lines. You'll want to use the back of the knife because you don't want to cut into your pastry.

9. Chill for thirty minutes or twenty-four hours.

10.   Heat your oven to 400, and then brush it with a little more egg yolk. Cook for twenty to twenty-five minutes, and then allow to stand for ten before slicing.

Pheasant on a Bed of Wild Rice

If you want to go traditional, then pheasant is the perfect main dish for your Christmas dinner. Serving it with wild rice on the side or as the bed for plating is a great pair, and this recipe will be both pleasing to the eyes and the taste buds.

Serves: 6-8

Time: 1 Hour 25 Minutes

Ingredients:

- 2 ½ Teaspoons Parsley Flakes, Dried
- 2 Teaspoons Sea Salt, Fine
- 2 2/3 Cup Water
- ¾ Cup Yellow Onion, Chopped
- 10.75 Ounces Condensed Cream of Mushroom Soup
- 2 Teaspoons Garlic Powder
- 2 Teaspoon Oregano, Dried
- 1 ½ Teaspoons Paprika
- 1 Tablespoon All Purpose Flour
- 1 Teaspoon Black Pepper
- 6 Bacon Strips, Chopped
- 1 Oven Roasting Bag, Large
- 2 Cups Wild Rice, Uncooked

- ½ lbs Mushrooms, Sliced & Freshed
- 4 lb Pheasant, Halved

Directions:

1. Start by combining your mushroom soup, water, onion, parsley, salt, garlic, oregano, paprika, and pepper together. Bring this mixture to a boil.
2. Place your flour in an oven bag, shaking to coat, and then place it in a 13x9 baking pan. Add in your bacon, and sprinkle your rice and mushrooms over the bacon. Add in your pheasant, and pour your mixture into the bag.
3. Cut six slits in the top of the bag. They should be one half inch, and then tie the bag closed.
4. Turn your oven to 350 and then bake for one to one and a half hours. Let stand for ten minutes before serving.

Brisket & Gravy

This is an old fashion meal that's been served as Christmas dinner for many families. If you've never enjoyed a brisket cooked to perfection with onion and mushroom gravy, then your next Christmas dinner is the perfect time to try!

Serves: 10-12

Time: 13 Hours 45 Minutes

Ingredients:

- 1 Tablespoon Garlic Powder
- 2 Tablespoons Sea Salt
- 2 ½ Teaspoons Black Pepper, Ground Fresh
- 1 Teaspoon Onion Powder
- 5 lbs Beef Brisket, Trimmed
- 1 Ounce Porcini Mushrooms, Dried

- 2 Cups Water, Boiling
- 2 Tablespoons Extra Virgin Olive Oil
- 2 Cups Beef Broth, Reduced Sodium
- 12 Garlic Cloves, Smashed
- 2 Sprigs Thyme, Fresh
- 2 Large Carrots, Cut Into 1 Inch Pieces
- ¼ Bunch Flat Leaf Parsley, Fresh
- 3 Large Yellow Onions
- 6 Tablespoons Butter, Divided
- 1 lb Cremini Mushrooms, Quartered
- 2 ½ Tablespoons Cornstarch

Directions:

1. Stir your salt, black pepper, garlic, and onion powder together. Rub it over your brisket, and then place it on a lined pan. Chill and cover for eight hours.
2. Let it stand for thirty minutes at room temperature, and then preheat your oven to 325.
3. Soak your porcini mushrooms in your boiling water for about ten minutes.
4. Coo your brisket for four minutes on each side in a Dutch oven. They should be browned, and then add in your broth, garlic cloves, carrot, thyme and parsley. Add in your porcini mushrooms, and then add the mushroom soaking liquid into the pan in your Dutch oven.
5. Cover it with a tight fitting lid, and then bake at 325 for four hours.
6. Let it stand for thirty minutes.
7. Thinly slice your onions and then melt your butter in a skillet over medium heat. Add in your onions and stir occasionally, cooking for fifteen minutes. It should become tender and golden, and then remove your onion from the skillet.
8. Increase your heat to medium-high, melting two more tablespoons of butter. Add in your cremini mushrooms, and then sauté for eight minutes. It should brown and become tender. Remove your cremini mushrooms, and then add them to your onion mixture.
9. Slice your brisket across the grain, and then put them on a serving platter.
10. Strain your cooking liquid, and then remove the solids.
11. Bring this liquid to a boil over medium-high heat, and then stir in your onion and mushroom mixture. Cook while stirring occasionally for about five minutes.

12.   Melt the remaining two tablespoons of butter in a pan over medium-high heat adding in your cornstarch. Make sure to whisk until smooth or it will clump.

13.   Cook and whisk for thirty seconds, making sure to whisk constantly.

14.   Add your cornstarch mix to your gravy, whisking to combine so it doesn't clump.

15.   Bring your gravy to boil, and cook like this for a full minute. Remove from heat, and then season with salt and pepper to taste.

16.   Place over your brisket and serve.

Sweet Bourbon Glazed Ham

If you want to use a fully cooked ham and give it an extra twist, then this is the perfect ham recipe for you! It'll taste like you did everything yourself, making the perfect Christmas entrée.

Serves: 12-15

Time: 3 Hours

Ingredients:

- 9 ¼ lb Fully Cooked Ham, Bone In
- 40 Cloves, Whole
- ½ Cup Light Brown Sugar, Firmly Packed
- ½ Cup Honey, Raw
- ½ Cup Bourbon
- 1/3 Cup Creole Mustard
- 1/3 Cup Molasses, Pure

Directions:

1. Heat your oven to 350, and then remove the skin from the ham and trim the fat. The fat should be about ¼ inch thickness. Make shallow cuts about an inch apart in a diamond pattern, inserting the cloves into it. Place it on a baking sheet.
2. Stir your honey, creole mustard, molasses and bourbon together with your brown sugar. Spoon it over your ham.
3. Bake on your lowest rack for about two hours and thirty minutes. You should baste it with the juices in your pan every thirty minutes. After an hour, you'll need to cover it.
4. Let it stand a half hour before serving.

Spiced Beef

Spiced beef is a delicacy that is served in many parts of Ireland, especially Cork. This traditional Irish dish takes time to prepare, but its well worth it.

Serves: 8-10

Time: 30 Minutes (Plus 6-7 Days for Marinating)

Ingredients:

- 6 ½ lbs Top Sirloin Roast
- 3 ½ Tablespoons Allspice Berries
- 1/3 Cup Dark Brown Sugar, Packed Firm
- 2 ½ Tablespoons Black Peppercorns
- 3 ½ Tablespoons Juniper Berries
- 1 Teaspoon Nutmeg, Freshly Grated
- 2 ½ Tablespoons Whole Cloves
- 1 Tablespoon Saltpeter
- 1/3 Cup Sea Salt, Fine
- 1 Turn, Peeled & Coarsely Chopped

Directions:

1. Start by trimming any excess fat from your beef. Rub the sugar into it, and then place in a bowl in your refrigerator. Leave it there for twelve hours.
2. Use a mortar and pestle the next day to grind your spices, saltpeter and salt together. Rub this spice mix and salt mix over your meat, recover and refrigerate for six to seven days, making sure to turn daily.
3. Transfer to a large saucepan with a heavy bottom, and then add in your turnips. Cover with cool water, and then bring it to a boil. Let it simmer for two hours, and lift into a serving dish. Serve cold.

Cherry Pork Loin

If you're on a budget but still want an amazing Christmas dinner, then this cherry and balsamic pork loin is the right combination of sweet and savory for a great dinner.

Serves: 6-8

Time: 3 Hours 25 Minutes

Ingredients:

- 1 Tablespoon Olive Oil
- ½ Cup Cherries, Dried
- 1/3 Cup Balsamic Vinegar
- ¼ Cup Dark Brown Sugar, Packed
- ½ Teaspoon Black Pepper
- ¾ Cup Cherry Preserves
- 1 Teaspoon Sea Salt, Fine
- 3-4 lbs Pork Loin Roast

Directions:

1. Start by sprinkling your pepper and salt over your roast. Brown the roast loin a skillet on all sides over medium-high heat.
2. Once browned, place it in a slow cooker. The slow cooker should be a six quart one or more.
3. Mix your cherries, preserves, balsamic vinegar, and brown sugar together.
4. Pour the blend over the roast, and cook on low for three to four hours. It should be tender, and you'll want to cover for this entire time.
5. Let stand for fifteen minutes before slicing.

Crusted Salmon

Some people prefer to have a seafood Christmas, making salmon a perfect choice. It's even more holiday seasoned with this dill and pecan crust, making it perfect for Christmas or Christmas Eve. The best part is that it'll be ready in about a half hour!

Serves: 10-12

Time: 30 Minutes

Ingredients:

- 1 ½ Cups Pecan Halves
- 2 Garlic Cloves, Minced
- 6 Tablespoons Butter, Melted
- 3 ½ lbs Salmon, Boneless & Skinless
- 1 ½ Teaspoons Dill Weed, Dried
- 1 ¼ Teaspoons Sea Salt
- ½ Teaspoon Ground Black Pepper, Fresh

Directions:

1. Start by heating your oven to 400.
2. Pulse your pecans, melted butter, dill weed and garlic together in a food processor until it resembles a coarse crumb.
3. Sprinkle this over your salmon, and then sprinkle your pepper and salt.
4. Place your salmon on a lined baking sheet, and then spread the pecan mixture over it.
5. Bake for eighteen to twenty minutes. The salmon should flake with a fork.

Crusted Rib Roast

This rib roast is crusted to give it extra texture to go along with the flavor, making it perfect for Christmas dinner.

Serves: 8

Time: 3 Hours 5 Minutes

Ingredients:

- 2 Teaspoons Fennel Seeds
- 2 Teaspoons Black Pepper
- 7-9 lbs Prime Rib Roast, Trimmed
- 1 Tablespoon Extra Virgin Olive Oil
- 1 ½ Teaspoons Coriander Seeds
- 4 Teaspoons Sea Salt

Directions:

1. Start by heating your oven to 400, and then let the roast stand for thirty minutes at room temperature.
2. Pulse your pepper, fennel, and coriander until fragrant.
3. Rub your roast with oil, and then sprinkle lit over with your sea salt. Press your mixture into all sides of the roast, placing it on your prepared roasting pan.
4. Bake for two hours, and then let stand for fifteen minutes to an hour before slicing.

Chapter 3: Christmas Side Dishes

Having the right side dish to go along with your main dish can be just as important when you're trying to impress your guests, and that's where this chapter comes in handy. You'll be able to cook a meal perfect for you from start to finish by picking any of these wonderful side dish recipes!

Cream Cheese Mashed Potatoes

Everyone loves a good mashed potato, especially if you pair it with a good gravy. If you're serving any traditional beef or pork, you'll want to pair it with this creamy mashed potato recipe.

Serves: 6-8

Time: 50 Minutes

Ingredients:

- 3 ½ lbs Russet Potatoes
- 1 ½ Teaspoon White Pepper
- 1 ½ Teaspoon Sea Salt, Fine
- Garlic Powder to Taste
- 8 Ounces Cream Cheese, Softened
- ½ Cup Unsalted Butter, Softened
- ½ Cup Heavy Cream, Warmed
- ¼ Cup Whole Milk, Warmed

Directions:

1. Start by peeling your potatoes.
2. Place them in a pot with a tablespoon of salt. Cover with cold water, and then bring it to a boil.
3. Once boiling, reduce the heat, and then cover your potatoes partially. Let them simmer until your potatoes are tender. This will take about thirty-five minutes.
4. Drain and let them cool until you can handle them.

5. Cut your potatoes into large pieces.
6. Add in your butter, milk, cream, and cream cheese. Mash or place in a food processor until smooth. Season with salt and pepper.
7. Return to the pot, and then add garlic as desired.

Simple Roasted Asparagus

If you like asparagus, then you'll love this classically roasted recipe.

Serves: 6-8

Time: 35 Minutes

Ingredients:

- 2 Tablespoons Lemon Juice, Fresh
- 3 lbs Asparagus Spears
- 2 Teaspoons Extra Virgin Olive Oil
- 1 Garlic Clove, Chopped
- Salt & Pepper to Taste

Directions:

1. Start by heating your oven to 400, and then cut the tough ends from your asparagus spears.
2. Toss your asparagus with two teaspoons of olive oil, a chopped garlic clove, and two tablespoons fresh lemon juice in a baking pan. Season with salt and pepper, and then roast for twenty-five to thirty minutes.
3. Serve warm.

Smooth Mac & Cheese

Mac and cheese is a classic favorite for many people, but this isn't your normal boxed recipe. You'll find that this recipe certainly brings the kid friendly dish to the adult table.

Serves: 6-8

Time: 1 Hour

Ingredients:

- 3 Tablespoons All Purpose Flour
- 2 ½ Cups Whole Milk
- 3 Tablespoons Butter
- 2 Shallots, Chopped Fine
- 32 Ounces Potato Gnocchi
- ¼ Cup + 2 ½ Teaspoons Sea Salt, Fine
- 2 Tablespoon Fresh Thyme Leaves, Finely Chopped
- 2 Tablespoons Dijon Mustard
- ¼ Teaspoon Hot Sauce
- 4 Ounces Sharp Cheddar Cheese, Grated
- 4 Ounces Extra Sharp White Cheddar, Grated
- Vegetable Cooking Spray

Directions:

1. Start by heating your oven to 375.
2. Fill a stockpot with three quarts of water, and cook your gnocchi as per package instructions.
3. Melt your butter in a large saucepan, and ten add in your shallots. Sauté for about thirty seconds or until your shallots become fragrant.
4. Add in your chopped thyme and flour, cooking and stirring constantly for two to three minutes. Your mixture should turn a golden brown, and it should become smooth.
5. Start to whisk in your milk, increasing the heat to high.
6. Bring your mix to a boil, and make sure to whisk occasionally. You'll want to bring it down to a simmer by reducing it to medium-low, whisking constantly for about five minutes. Your sauce should thicken slightly, and then stir in your mustard and hot sauce. Remove it from heat.
7. Add in your cheeses, and stir until melted.
8. Add in your salt, and then transfer to a pan that's been lightly greased.
9. Bake at 375 for about twenty to twenty-five minutes. It should be golden and bubbly, and then broil for two minutes until browned. Serve warm.

Creamy Brussel Sprouts

Parmesan really brings out a unique taste with this Brussel sprouts recipe. This recipe goes great with any type of poultry.

Serves: 6-8

Time: 55 Minutes

Ingredients:

- 3 lbs Brussel Sprouts
- 2 Teaspoons Sea Salt, Fine
- 1 ½ Tablespoons Extra Virgin Olive Oil
- 3 Fresh Rosemary Sprigs
- 4-6 Garlic Cloves
- 2 Cups Heavy Cream
- 11/2 Teaspoon Ground Black Pepper
- ¼ Cup Parmesan Cheese, Freshly Grated

Directions:

1. Start by heating your oven to 425.
2. Toss your Brussel sprouts in olive oil, salt and half a teaspoon of your black pepper. Layer them on a baking sheet, baking for twenty-five minutes.
3. Stir your cream, garlic and rosemary together in a saucepan. Cook over medium heat for about twenty minutes. It should reduce to about one cup and you'll need to stir occasionally.
4. Discard your garlic and rosemary, and then stir in your grated cheese.
5. Drizzle over your Brussel sprouts, and top with more cheese or chives if desired.

Walnut & Citrus Salad

Salad is sometimes the best side dish, especially if you're looking for something healthy to serve. However, that doesn't mean it has to be boring!

Serves: 6-8

Time: 30 Minutes

Ingredients:

- ½ Cup Walnut Pieces
- ½ Cup Parsley Leaves, Fresh & Packed Firm
- 8 Heads Belgian Endive
- 2 Red Grapefruits, Sectioned & Peeled

Directions:

1. Start by heating your oven to 350, and then bake your walnuts until fragrant and lightly toasted. It should take six to eight minutes. Make sure to stir halfway through.

2. Prepare your endive by removing the outer leaves, and then rinse in cold water before patting dry. Cut each head diagonally. You should make quarter inch slices, and then place them in a serving bowl.
3. Add your parsley and walnuts, and then add your desired dressing.
4. Toss gently before topping with grapefruit, and serve.

Garlic Green Beans

If you're looking for something simple and complimentary to most entrees, then garlic green beans can be your go to side dish.

Serves: 12-16

Time: 25 Minutes

Ingredients:

- 2 Teaspoons Sea Salt, Fine
- ½ Teaspoon Ground Black Pepper
- 2 Tablespoons Extra Virgin Olive Oil
- 3-4 Large Garlic Cloves, Sliced Thin
- 3 lbs Green Beans, Trimmed

Directions:

1. Start by cooking your beans in salted water until tender. This should take about five minutes, and then you'll need to drain them.
2. Cook half of your garlic in a tablespoon of oil until golden, and then add in half of your green beans. Toss with a half teaspoon of salt and a quarter teaspoon of pepper, cooking for three minutes while stirring constantly.
3. Transfer to a serving dish and repeat the procedure.
4. Serve warm.

Roasted Winter Vegetables

This is a more traditional recipe from when people ate with the seasons. With the taste of cranberry added in, you'll find that this side dish is even more seasonal!

Serves: 6-8

Time: 1 Hour 5 Minutes

Ingredients:

- 1 ½ lbs Carrots (about 4 Large Carrots), Halved Lengthwise & Cut into 1 Inch Pieces
- 1 lb Brussel Sprouts, Quartered or Halved
- 3 Large Turnips, Peeled & Cut Into 1 Inch Pieces
- 2 Teaspoons Extra Virgin Olive Oil
- ¾ Teaspoon Sea Salt, Fine
- 1 Tablespoon Rosemary, Fresh & Minced
- 1 Cup Fresh Cranberries (Or thawed if frozen)
- 4 Teaspoons Molasses

Directions:

1. Start by heating your oven to 400.
2. Grease two large pans, placing your turnips and carrots in one.
3. Place your Brussel sprout sin your second pan, and divide your rosemary, olive oil, salt and pepper between both pans. Toss to coat.
4. Bake both pans at 400 for thirty minutes, making sure to stir once.
5. Add in your cranberries, baking for five more minutes. Your cranberries should begin to soften, and your carrots and turnips should be tender and lightly browned.
6. Bake your Brussel sprouts until tender and browned as well.
7. Remove them from the oven, and then drizzle with molasses.

Spice Glazed Carrots

You'll need a vegetable with your dessert, and these spice glazed carrots are the perfect addition to your Christmas dinner.

Serves: 6-8

Time: 1 Hour

Ingredients:

- ½ Cup Orange Marmalade
- 2 Tablespoons Extra Virgin Olive Oil
- 1 Teaspoon Ground Cumin
- 1 ¾ lbs Carrots
- ½ Cup Orange Juice
- 1 Teaspoon Ground Ginger
- 1 Teaspoon Sea Salt, Fine
- 1 Teaspoon Rosemary Leaves, Fresh & Minced
- ¼ Teaspoon Crushed Red Pepper, Dried
- 1 Teaspoon Black Pepper

Directions:

1. Start by heating your oven to 475, and then cut the tops from your carrots. You may want to leave an inch of greenery on each. Peel your carrots, and then toss them in a large bowl.
2. Sprinkle your cumin and salt over them, spraying a baking sheet and spreading your carrots over it in a single layer. Bake for about twenty-five minutes. Your carrots should be lightly browned and tender.
3. Bring your orange juice, ginger and marmalade to a boil in a small pan over medium heat. Stir often for four to six minutes. It should thicken, and then stir in your rosemary.
4. Transfer your carrots to a bowl, and then toss them in your marmalade mixture.
5. Season with pepper to taste, and then serve warm.

Braised Cabbage & Bacon

The bacon may have been what caught your interest with this side dish recipe, but cabbage has never tasted so good!

Serves: 6-8

Time: 1 Hour 20 Minutes

Ingredients:

- 4-6 Thick Bacon Slices, Cut in ¼ Inch Pieces

- 4 Celery Hearts, sliced Thin with Leaves Reserved
- 1 Medium Yellow Onion, Sliced Thin
- 2 Teaspoons Fennel Seeds
- 1 Head Red Cabbage, Thinly Sliced (about 2 lbs)
- ½ Cup White Wine
- 1 Cup Chicken Broth, Reduced Sodium
- 1 Cup Apple Cider, Unfiltered
- 1-2 Garlic Cloves, Sliced Thin
- 1 Tart Apple, Sliced Thin
- 2-3 Bay Leaves
- 1 Tablespoon Apple Cider Vinegar

Directions:

1. Start by cooing your bacon until crisp. Remove the bacon from your pan and drain, reserving three tablespoons of dripping.
2. Turn your heat up to medium-high, and then add in your celery, fennel seeds and onion. Sauté this blend for six minutes, and then add in your wine cooking until it reduces by half. This should take about two minutes.
3. Stir in your cabbage, chicken broth, garlic, bay leaves, apple cider and apple. Season with salt and pepper according to your tastes.
4. Reduce the heat to low, and then cook for forty-five minutes while covered. Stir in your remaining vinegar, and then top with bacon and celery leaves.

Glazed Parsnips & Turnips

Glazed vegetables make a sweet treat for your Christmas dinner, and these winter vegetables make the perfect addition to your meal.

Serves: 6-8

Time: 1 Hour

Ingredients:

- 1-2 Bay Leaves
- 2 Teaspoons Sea Salt, Fine
- 1 ½ Cups Pearl Onions, Frozen
- 2 lbs Turnips, Peeled & Cut (Into ½ Inch Wedges)

- 1 lb Parsnips, Peeled & Cut (Into ½ Inch Wedges)
- 3 Tablespoons Cane Vinegar, Divided
- 2 Tablespoons Extra Virgin Olive Oil
- 2 Tablespoons Butter
- 3 Inch Cinnamon Stick
- ¼ Teaspoon Crushed Red Pepper, Dried
- ½ Cup Vegetable Broth
- ¾ Cup Cane Syrup

Directions:

1. Start by bringing your turnips, parsnips, pearl onions and salt to a boil adding a tablespoon of your vinegar and water. Stir occasionally and cook until your vegetables are tender, making sure to drain afterwards.
2. Cook your butter, olive oil, cinnamon, red pepper and bay leaf together over medium heat, stirring for about a minute. The butter should melt and the spices should become fragrant.
3. Add in your turnip mixture, sautéing in your butter mix for eight to ten minutes. They should become browned and tender, discard your cinnamon stick and bay leaf.
4. Stir in your cane sugar, broth and your remaining vinegar. Cook while stirring often until your mix thickens and your vegetables are coated. This should take eight to ten minute, and then add salt to taste.

Potato Gratin

Fennel and nutmeg spice up this potato gratin to make it ready for your Christmas table.

Serves: 6-8

Time: 1 Hour 25 Minutes

Ingredients:

- 3 Tablespoons Butter
- 2 Garlic Cloves, Minced
- 1 Shallot, Sliced Thin
- 1 ¼ Cups Half & Half
- 10 Ounces Sharp White Cheddar, Shredded

- 2 Tablespoons All Purpose Flour
- ¼ Teaspoon Black Pepper
- 1/8 Teaspoon Nutmeg, Ground
- 2lbs Baking Potato, Peeled & Sliced Thin (about 2 Large potatoes)
- 1 Small Fennel Bulb, Sliced Thin
- Rosemary Sprigs for Garnish

Directions:

1. Start by heating your oven to 400, and then melt your butter in a saucepan over medium heat. Add in your shallots, sautéing for two to three minutes. The shallots should become tender before adding your garlic and sautéing for about a minute more. The garlic should become fragrant.
2. Whisk in your flour, cooking for about one minute while whisking constantly to make sure it doesn't clump.
3. Start by whisking your half and half in gradually, cooing for three to four minutes until it starts to bubble and become thick. Stir in your salt, pepper and nutmeg.
4. Layer your potato and fennel slices in an alternating pattern. It should be lightly greased and broiler safe.
5. Spread your cheese over your layers, and then cover with foil.
6. Cook for about fifty minutes or until your potatoes are tender.
7. Remove them from the oven and then increase the temperature to broil. Uncover and broil for two to four minutes. It should turn a golden brown before garnishing and serving.

Brussel Sprouts & Apples

Apples may not sound like they go to Brussel sprouts, but the pairing elevates this side dish to the next level of delightful tastes.

Serves: 4-6

Time: 35 Minutes

Ingredients:

- 1 ½ lbs Brussel Sprouts, Trimmed
- 1 Braeburn Apple, Peeled & Diced
- 4-6 Bacon Slices

- 2 Tablespoons Shallots, Minced
- ¼ Cup White Wine, Dry
- 1 Garlic Clove, Minced
- ¼ Cup Chicken Broth, Low Sodium
- 1 Teaspoon Sea Salt, Fine
- ½ Teaspoon Black Pepper
- ¼ Cup Parmesan Cheese, Freshly Grated

Directions:

1. Cut your Brussel sprouts in half, and then cut into shreds.
2. Cook your bacon until crisp, and then drain on a paper towel. Reserve three tablespoons of your drippings, crumbling.
3. Sauté your shallots, garlic, hot drippings and apple together over medium-high heat. After about three minutes stir in your white wine, chicken broth and salt and pepper. Bring it to a boil before reducing heat.
4. Allow to simmer for about five more minutes, and then sauté for eight to ten minutes.
5. Your Brussel sprouts should become tender and crisp. Top with your crumbled bacon and cheese before serving.

Lively Green Beans

These green beans are spiced up with crushed red pepper, making them have a bit more livelily of a taste to add to your Christmas dinner.

Serves: 6-8

Time: 20 Minutes

Ingredients:

- 2lbs Green Beans, Fresh & Trimmed
- 3 Cups Shitake Mushrooms, Sliced
- ¼ Cup Shallots, Chopped
- 8-10 Bacon Slices
- 1/8 -1/4 Teaspoon Crushed Red Pepper, Dried
- ¼ Teaspoon Sea Salt, Fine
- ½ Teaspoon Ground Black Pepper

Directions:

1. Start by boiling your green beans in salt water. They should be crisp but tender, and then you'll need to drain them.
2. Plunge them into ice water and then drain. Set these green beans aside.
3. Cook your bacon until crisp, and then drain on a paper towel. Reserve one and a half tablespoons of your bacon drippings. Discard anything else, and then crumble your bacon.
4. Sauté your shallots and mushrooms for five minutes over medium-high heat. They should become tender, and then add in your crushed red pepper and green beans. Continue to sauté for one to two minutes. Stir in your bacon, and then your black pepper and sea salt.

Sweet Potato Casserole

This is a classic dish that's often served on Christmas. It adds a sweet and tender side that goes great with any poultry dish.

Serves: 6-8

Time: 2 Hours 40 Minutes

Ingredients:

- 1 Cup White Sugar
- 4 ½ lbs Sweet Potatoes
- 2 Large Eggs
- ¼ Cup Whole Milk
- ½ Cup Butter, Softened
- 1 Teaspoon Vanilla Extract, Pure
- 1 ¼ Cups Cornflake Cereal, Crushed
- ¼ Teaspoon Sea Salt, Fine
- ¼ Cup Pecans, Chopped
- 1 Tablespoon Light Brown Sugar

- 1 ½ Cups Marshmallows, Miniature
- 1 Tablespoon Butter, Melted

Directions:

1. Start by heating your oven to 400.
2. Bake your sweet potatoes until tender, and it'll take about an hour.
3. Let it stand for twenty minutes, and then peel them and mash them. Reduce your oven to 350.
4. Add your sugar and mash your sweet potatoes. Add in your butter, milk, eggs, salt, and vanilla. Make sure to mix until smooth.
5. Put the mixture in an 11x7 baking dish that's been lightly greased.
6. Mix your pecans, brown sugar, melted butter and cornflakes together before spreading them over your casserole.
7. Bake for about a half hour, and then remove from the oven. Let it cool for ten minutes before sprinkling your marshmallows on top, and bake for another ten minutes before serving once cooled.

Baked Onions

This is a simple country dish that goes with almost any main dish that you'll be serving for Christmas. These onions are sweetened and caramelized to make the perfect side.

Serves: 4-6

Time: 1 Hour

Ingredients:

- 30 Ounces Pearl Onions
- ¼ Cup Butter
- 5 Teaspoons Light Brown Sugar
- ¾ Teaspoon Sea Salt, Fine
- ½ Teaspoon Cracked Black Pepper
- 3-4 Garlic Cloves, Chopped
- 1/3 Cup White Wine, Dry

Directions:

1. Start by heating your oven to 425.

2. Boil your onions for about three minutes before draining. Rinse them under cold water before letting them stand for about five minutes.
3. Cut the root off of one of your onion ends, and then squeeze the end of the onion toward the root, which will remove the outer peel. Discard this peel.
4. Melt your butter, and then stir in your onion. Transfer to a baking pan.
5. Bake for fifteen minutes, and then stir in your wine, salt, cloves, pepper and brown sugar.
6. Bake for thirty-five to forty minutes.

Classic Butterbeans

If you're from the south, then you've probably grown up with butterbeans as a side dish for any holiday. This classic recipe brings a taste of the south to your table for a delicious meal.

Serves: 6-8

Time: 2 Hours 10 Minutes

Ingredients:

- ½ Cup Light Brown Sugar, Packed Firm
- 16 Ounces Frozen Butterbeans
- ¼ Cup Butter
- 1 Small Yellow Onion, Minced
- 5-7 Slices Bacon, Diced
- 2 Teaspoons Sea Salt, Fine
- 1 Teaspoon Cracked Black Pepper

Directions:

1. Cook your bacon and onion together over medium heat for five to seven minutes before adding in your brown sugar. Make sure to stir, and keep cooking until your sugar is dissolved. It should take one to two minutes.
2. Stir in your butterbeans, adding in your butter until melted and your beans are coated. You'll want to add twelve cups of water now.
3. Bring it to a boil over medium-high heat before reducing it to a simmer. Stir occasionally, cooking for two hours. The beans should

become tender, and your liquid should thicken to just below your beans. Stir in your pepper and salt before serving.

Homemade Crescent Rolls

Sometimes you just want to make something from scratch to add to a special dinner. That's where this homemade recipe comes in handy.

Yields: 12

Time: 1 Hour 40 Minutes

Ingredients:

- ¾ Cup Warm Water
- ¼ Ounce Active Dry Yeast
- 2 Tablespoons White Sugar
- 3 ½ Cups All Purpose Baking Mix
- All Purpose Flour

Directions:

1. Start by combining your yeast and warm water. Let it stand for about five minutes.
2. Combine three cups of your baking mix with your sugar, gradually stirring in your yeast mix.
3. Turn your dough onto a floured surface, and then knead it. Add additional baking mix as needed. The dough should become elastic and smooth, but this will take about ten minutes.
4. Roll your dough into a twelve inch circle, cutting it into twelve wedges.
5. Roll the wedges up, but make sure to start at the wide end if you want to roll them right. Make the crescent shape, and then lightly grease your baking sheet. Cover and let rise in a warm place for about an hour.
6. Preheat your oven to 425, baking for ten to twelve minutes. They should be golden brown. Serve warm.

Cheesy Squash Casserole

Parmesan and cheddar go great together in this squash casserole. If you want to be a little different, substitute half of your squash for zucchini to make a slightly more colorful dish.

Serves: 10-12

Time: 45 Minutes

Ingredients:

- 4 lbs Yellow Squash, Sliced
- 1 Large Sweet Onion, Chopped Fine
- 4 Ounces Cheddar Cheese, Shredded (about 1 Cup)
- 2 Tablespoons Butter, Melted
- 1 ¼ Cup Parmesan Cheese, Divided (5 Ounces)
- 2 ½ Cups Breadcrumbs, Fresh & Divided
- 1 Teaspoon Ground Black Pepper, Fresh
- 2 Large Eggs, Beaten Lightly
- 8 Ounces Sour Cream
- ½ Cup Fresh Chives, Chopped
- 1 Teaspoon Garlic Salt

Directions:

1. Start by heating your oven to 350.
2. Boil your yellow squash and onion until tender. Drain this mixture.
3. Combine your squash mix and cheddar together. Add in your chives, sour cream, pepper, salt and eggs. Mix well before adding one cup of your breadcrumbs and ¾ cup of your parmesan cheese, spooning it into a baking dish that's been lightly greased. It's best to use a 13x9 inch baking dish.
4. Stir your remaining parmesan, breadcrumbs and melted butter together. Top your casserole with this mixture.
5. Bake at 350. It should take about thirty-five to forty minutes to set.

Spiced Honey Citrus Salad

This is a unique but somewhat traditional Christmas side dish that is often served with goose or duck.

Serves: 6-8

Time: 1 Hour 5 Minutes

Ingredients:

- ¼ Teaspoon Crushed Red Pepper, Dried
- 1 Bay Leaf
- 1 Teaspoon Black Peppercorns
- ½ Cup Honey
- 4 Cloves, Whole
- 3 Medium Oranges
- 3 Mandarin Oranges
- 2 Red Grapefruits
- 2 Limes
- 3 Inch Cinnamon Stick
- 6 Kumquats (Optional)
- 4.4 Ounces Pomegranate Seeds, Fresh
- Mint for Topping

Directions:

1. Take a half a cup of water, cinnamon, honey, bay leaf, peppercorns, cloves and red pepper together to a boil over medium-high heat.
2. Boil, but make sure to stir often for one minute. Then remove it from heat, letting stand a half hour.
3. Peel your oranges, mandarin oranges, red grapefruit and limes. Peel your kumquats if you're using them as well but cut away the bitter pith. Your fruit should be cut in thin rounds, and then arrange on a serving platter, sprinkling with your pomegranate seeds.
4. Pour your honey mixture through a strainer, discarding solids, and then drizzle your fruit with it.
5. Top with your mint leaves.

Simple House Rolls

If you don't want to go with crescents, then you might want to try this simple roll recipe to bring buttery flavor to your table.

Yields: 36

Time: 7 Hours 10 Minutes

Ingredients:

- 1 Envelope Active Dry Yeast
- 1 ½ Teaspoons Sea Salt, Fine
- 1 Large Egg, Room Temperature
- ¼ Cup Unsalted Butter
- Flakey Sea Salt
- Canola Oil
- 3 Tablespoons White Sugar
- 1 Cup Whole Milk
- ¼ Cup Vegetable Shortening
- 3 ½ Cups All Purpose Flour (Plus More for Your Surface)

Directions:

1. Whisk your yeast and a quarter cup of warm water in a bowl, letting it stand for five minutes.
2. Heat your milk over medium heat in a small saucepan until its warm. Add in your shortening, sugar and sea salt in a bowl. Not your flakey sea salt.
3. Whisk to blend, adding in your warm milk and breaking you're shortening into small clumps. It may not completely melt, but you can still whisk in your egg and yeast mix. Add in your flour, and stir with a wooden spoon. You'll need to stir vigorously until your dough forms.
4. Knead your dough with floured hands on a floured surface until smooth. This will take about four to five minutes, and then you'll need to transfer into a lightly oiled bowl, turning to coat.
5. Cover with plastic wrap loosely, and let it sit at room temperature until doubled. This will take about one and a half hours.
6. Heat your oven to 350, and then melt your butter.
7. Lightly brush your baking dish with the butter, and punch down your dough. You'll want to divide your dough into four equal pieces.
8. Roll out each piece at a time into a rectangle that's 12 by 6 inches.

9. Cut into two inch wide strips, which should give you three. Cut each strip crosswise, making three four inch by two inch rectangles.
10.   Brush half of each of these smaller rectangles with your melted butter, and then fold your unbuttered side over. You'll need about a quarter inch of overhang.
11.   Place flat in a corner of your dish, folding your edge against the short side of your baking dish.
12.   Add your remaining rolls to form one long row. Brush with melted butter and then cover loosely with plastic wrap, chilling for at least thirty minutes and up to six hours.
13.   Bake for twenty-five to thirty-five minutes. They should become golden and puffed, and then brush with butter and sprinkle with your flaky sea salt.

Country Corn Casserole

If you're looking for a true country dish, you'll want to try this corn casserole in all its cheesy goodness.

Serves: 6-8

Time: 1 Hour 10 Minutes

Ingredients:

- 15.25 Ounces Whole Kernel Corn, Canned & Drained
- 14.75 Ounces Cream Style Corn, Canned
- 8 Ounces Corn Muffin Mix Package
- 1 Cup Sour Cream
- ½ Stick Butter, Melted
- 1 ½ Cups Cheddar, Shredded

Directions:

1. Start by heating your oven to 350.
2. Stir both your corns, corn muffin mix, sour cream and butter together before pouring it into a lightly greased casserole dish. It's best to use a nine by thirteen inch dish, and then bake for forty-five minutes. It should turn a golden brown.

3. Remove from the oven, topping with your cheddar before baking for five to ten more minutes. Your cheese should be melted, and you'll want to let it stand for five minutes before serving.

Lemon Roasted Cauliflower

Don't let the time frame scare you on this simple and easy side dish recipe! You simply need to make your dressing at least four hours in advance to let it properly marinate and chill.

Serves: 4

Time: 4 Hours 40 Minutes

Ingredients:

- 6 Tablespoons Olive Oil, Divided
- ½ Teaspoon Lemon Zest, Finely Grated
- 2 Tablespoons Lemon Juice, Fresh
- 1 Cup Fresh Flat Leaf Parsley
- 2 lbs Cauliflower, Cut into Florets (Including the tender leaves)
- Salt & Pepper to Taste

Directions:

1. Pulse your parsley and lemon juice with two tablespoons of oil until chopped fine. Season with salt and pepper to taste, and then toss your cauliflower into it before serving with lemon zest as your topping.
2. Start by heating your oven to 425, and then toss your cauliflower in four tablespoons of oil. Season with salt and pepper to taste, rand then roast for twenty-five to thirty minutes until golden brown.

Roasted Butternut Squash

With spicy onions, this roasted butternut squash dish is great to add a little bit of kick to your holiday spread.

Serves: 8

Time: 45 Minutes

Ingredients:

- 2 Teaspoons Honey, Raw
- ¼ Cup Lime Juice, Fresh
- 1 Teaspoon Lime Zest, Finely Grated
- 1 Teaspoon Crushed Red Pepper Flakes, Dried
- 1 Medium Red Onion, Sliced
- 2 Tablespoons Extra Virgin Olive Oil
- 1 Cup Hazelnuts, Blanched
- 4lbs Butternut Squash, Seeded, Peeled & Sliced (1/4 Inch Thick Slices)
- ¼ Cup + 2 Tablespoons Extra Virgin Olive Oil
- Salt and Pepper to Taste
- ½ Cup Fresh Mint, Chopped
- ½ Cup Flat Leaf Parsley, Fresh & Chopped
- 2 Tablespoons Marjoram, Fresh & Chopped
- 4 Ounces Goat Cheese, Fresh & Crumbled

Directions:

1. You'll need to start by heating oil in a large skillet. Turn the heat to medium-high, and cook your onion while stirring often. You'll want to lightly char and soften them without letting your onions fall apart. This will take five to seven minutes.
2. Add in your red pepper flakes, tossing to combine, and then remove them from the pan.
3. Add in your lime juice and honey, stirring and let cool. Add in your lime zest as its cooling.
4. Turn your oven to 350, and then toast your hazelnuts until golden brown. This should take six to eight minutes. Once they cool, then coarsely chop your hazelnuts.
5. Turn the oven up to 400, and then toss your squash in a quarter cup of your olive oil. Season with salt and pepper to taste, and then divide the mix between two baking sheets.
6. Roast without stirring until tender, which should take fifteen to twenty minutes.
7. Return your squash to the bowl, adding in your marjoram, spicy onions, parsley, hazelnuts and mint. Toss to combine your ingredients.
8. Transfer the mix onto a serving platter, and crumble your goat cheese as a topping, drizzling your remaining two tablespoons of oil on top as well.

Roasted Chestnuts

Roasted chestnuts can be a great side dish or snack for Christmas, but you don't need an open fire to roast them properly. This tasty recipe is done in an oven.

Serves: 6-8

Time: 1 Hour 10 Minutes

Ingredients:

- 2 Teaspoons Sea Salt, Fine
- ½ Teaspoon Grated Nutmeg, Fresh
- ¼ Teaspoon Black Pepper
- ½ Cup (1 Stick) Butter, Unsalted & Melted
- 2-3 Sprigs Rosemary, Fresh
- 2 lbs Chestnuts, Fresh & Unshelled

Directions:

1. Start by turning your oven to 425, and then place a large sheet of foil on your baking sheet. The flat side of your chestnuts should be facing down, and then cut through the shell to score an x
2. Soak these chestnuts in a bowl of hot water for about one minute, which will help to steam them while they're roasting.
3. Drain your chestnuts, patting them dry before placing them in a bowl.
4. Add in your butter, sea salt, nutmeg and rosemary.
5. Season with pepper to taste, and arrange your chestnuts on the foil.
6. Fold the foil around your chestnuts, but leave an opening at the very top.
7. Roast until the peel starts to curl, and your chestnuts should be cooked all the way through. This will take about thirty to forty-five minutes.
8. Transfer them to a platter, tossing them in the butter and spices, and season with more salt if desired. Serve hot or at least warm.

Old fashioned Collard Green Gratin

If you don't want to go with collard greens despite them being more traditional, you may want to trade it to for curly Kale. Tuscan kale will work as well.

Serves: 6-8

Time: 1 Hour 5 Minutes

Ingredients:

- 1 Cup Parmesan, Grated Fine & Divided
- 1 Teaspoon Fresh Thyme, Chopped
- 1 Cup Breadcrumbs, Fresh & Coarse
- 4 Ounces Prosciutto, Thinly Sliced
- Sea Salt and Black Pepper to Taste
- 4 Tablespoons Extra Virgin Olive Oil, Divided
- 2 Tablespoons Butter, Unsalted
- 2 Cups Whole Milk
- ¼ Teaspoon Nutmeg, Freshly Grated
- 2 Tablespoons All Purpose Flour
- 1 Large Onion, Sliced Thin
- 2-3 Garlic Cloves, Finely Chopped
- 1 lb Collard Greens, Center Ribs & Stems Removed

Directions:

1. Turn your oven to 325, and then place your prosciutto on a baking sheet until crisp. It'll take twenty to twenty-five minutes until it becomes crisp.
2. Let it cool before breaking into small pieces.
3. Combine two tablespoons of your oil with your breadcrumbs, tossing them and then putting them in a skillet over medium heat. Make sure that you toss occasionally, cooking until brown and crisp which will take roughly ten minutes.
4. Add your thyme, ¼ cup of your Parmesan, salt and pepper after removing it from heat. Mix in your prosciutto next before setting it aside.
5. Boil your collard greens in salted water until bright green a tender, which will take about four minutes. Drain your collard greens and put them in a bowl of ice water to cool. Drain again, and then squeeze dry with a paper towel.

6. Chop them coarsely, and then take another saucepan and heat your remaining oil. Cook in your garlic and onion, stirring often. They should soften and turn golden, but it'll take about fifteen to twenty minutes. Transfer this to a bowl with your greens and then set it aside.
7. Turn your oven up to 400, and then melt your butter in a saucepan over medium-high heat.
8. Add in your flour and whisk constantly until it becomes a pale brown and smooth mixture. This will take three to four minutes.
9. Now gradually add in your milk and nutmeg, bringing it to a boil before reducing the heat to let it simmer. Whisk often for about five to eight minutes, and in this time it should thicken.
10. Whisk in your remaining parmesan, and then add in your collard green mix. Season with salt and pepper to taste.
11. Transfer to a skillet and top with your breadcrumbs. Bake for fifteen to twenty minutes before serving once it's cooled.

Nutmeg Popovers

This is a type of popover bread that makes a savory dinner roll, but they can be used as a salty snack too.

Yields: 12

Time: 45 Minutes

Ingredients:

- 2 Tablespoons Parsley, Chopped Fine
- 1 Tablespoon Sea Salt, Fine
- 1 Teaspoon Nutmeg, Finely Grated
- 2 Cups All Purpose Flour
- 3 Large Eggs
- 2 ½ Cups Whole Milk
- 1 Teaspoon Black Pepper, Freshly Grated
- 5 Tablespoons Unsalted Butter, Melted & Divided

Directions:

1. Whisk your parsley, salt, pepper, nutmeg and flour together.

2. Next, whisk in your eggs and whole milk in another bowl until blended. Make sure to whisk your flour mixture in, and then add in three tablespoons of your butter. Make sure that you don't overmix.
3. Turn your oven to 425, and then grease your muffin cups with the rest of your butter.
4. Pour the batter into your muffin tins, making sure there three quarters full and divide equally.
5. Bake until puffed, golden brown and crispy around the edges, which will take about thirty to thirty-five minutes.
6. Serve while warm.

Roasted Sweet Potatoes

These sweet potatoes have gotten to the next level with garlic and chile, giving them a sweetly spiced flavor.

Serves: 4

Time: 50 Minutes

Ingredients:

- 1 Teaspoon Hot Chili Sauce
- 1 Garlic Clove, Grated
- Sea Salt to Taste
- 2 Tablespoons Extra Virgin Olive Oil
- 1 ½ lbs Garnet Yams, Cut into ½ Inch Wedges

Directions:

1. Start by heating your oven to 425.
2. Toss your yams, seasoning with salt.
3. Roast until tender and browned in some spots. This should take about thirty-five to forty minutes.
4. Remove from the oven, tossing them in your hot chili sauce while still warm. Toss with garlic as well, and re-season with salt as desired.

Classic Sausage Stuffing

If you don't like gizzards in your stuffing, you may still like this classic protein filled stuffing blend. It's easy to make too!

Serves: 6-8

Time: 40 Minutes

Ingredients:

- 2 Onions, Chopped
- 1 Fennel Bulb, Chopped
- 10 Cups Torn Sourdough, Dried Out Overnight
- 1/3 Cup Hazelnuts, Blanched
- 3 Tablespoons Extra Virgin Olive Oil
- 4 Celery Stalks, Chopped
- Sea Salt & Pepper to taste
- ½ Cup White Wine, Dry
- 2 Large Eggs, Beaten to Blend

- 2 Cups Chicken Stock + More
- 1 ½ Sticks Unsalted Butter, Cut & Divided + More
- 12 Ounces Hot Italian Sausage, Casings Removed

Directions:

1. Start by heating your oven to 350, and then take a three quart baking dish and butter it as well as a sheet of foil. Place your bread in a large bowl.
2. Toast your hazelnuts on the baking sheet, tossing once until golden brown. This should take about ten to fifteen minutes, and chop them coarsely on they're cooled. Toss them into the bowl that has your bread.
3. Add your sausage to an oiled skillet over medium-high heat, and stir occasionally. Make sure to break it into small pieces. It should be cooked all the way through, which will take about seven to ten minutes. Transfer to your bread bowl using a slotted spoon.
4. Add in your fennel, sage, celery and onions to your skillet before seasoning with salt and pepper. Stir often as you cook, and your onions should turn golden brown. It should take ten to twelve minutes, and then transfer into the bowl with your bread.
5. Cook your wine in your skillet once you reduce your heat to medium, and then scrape any brown bits up. It should take about one minute, and most of it will evaporate. Add a half cup of your butter, and stir and cook until melted. Drizzle this over your bread mixture.
6. Whisk in your chicken stock and eggs, and then pour over your bread mix too.
7. Season with salt and pepper before tossing and add more stock one quarter cup at a time. Mix until combined and the bread is hydrated without being soaked. Add in your remaining quarter cup of butter, and then transfer to a baking dish.
8. Cover it with foil, and bake for thirty to thirty-five minutes. A knife inserted in the center should come out clean.
9. Uncover and then bake until the top is crisp and golden, which will take about twenty to twenty-five minutes.
10. Let sit for ten minutes before serving.

Classic Green Bean Casserole

Most people have had at least one green bean casserole before, and chances are you liked it. Your country Christmas dinner wouldn't be complete without it.

Serves: 6-8

Time: 50 Minutes

Ingredients:

- 1 Medium Onion, Cut into ¼ Inch Dice
- 1 Red Bell Pepper, Seeded & Cut into ½ Inch Dice
- 2 Teaspoons Coarse Sea Salt
- 6 Tablespoons All Purpose Flour
- ½ Teaspoon Black Pepper, Ground Fresh
- 1 lb Button mushrooms, Stems Trimmed & Quartered
- 6 Tablespoons Unsalted Butter + More
- 1 ½ lbs Green Beans, Trimmed & Cut into 2 Inch Pieces
- 2 Cups Whole Milk
- ½ Teaspoon Cayenne Pepper
- ½ Teaspoon Nutmeg, Grated Fresh
- 1 Cup Parmesan, Grated
- 4 Shallots, Cut into ¼ Inch Rings Cut Crosswise
- ¼ Cup Extra Virgin Olive Oil
- ¼ Cup Breadcrumbs

Directions:

1. Start by melting two tablespoons of butter over medium heat and then add in your onion. It should take about four minutes until it softens, and then add your bell pepper and mushrooms. Cook until softened, and most of the liquid should evaporate which will take about eight minutes. Season with salt and pepper to taste before setting it aside.
2. Prepare an ice bath, and set this aside. Boil a saucepan of water, and then add your beans, cooking until they're tender and bright green. It should take about four to five minutes, and then drain them before plunging them into your ice bath. Let them cool and toss them, draining before adding to your mushroom mixture.
3. Melt four tablespoons of butter over medium low heat, and then add a quarter cup of your flour, whisking constantly. The mixture should turn golden brown in about two minutes, and then pour in your milk as you

continue to whisk. The mixture should thicken n about three minutes before you stir in your salt, pepper, nutmeg and cayenne. Remove the mixture from heat, letting it cool to room temperature. Make sure to stir occasionally, and then pour it over your green beans tossing it to combine.

4. Butter a pan, 9x13 is recommended, and then spread half the green bean mixture at the bottom. Sprinkle half of your parmesan before adding the rest of your green beans. Combine your remaining parmesan and breadcrumbs before sprinkling it over the casserole. Cover with foil, and refrigerate until you're ready to finish.

5. Heat your oil over medium-high heat, and then toss your shallot rings with two tablespoons of flour. Fry them in batches, making them golden brown. You'll need to turn frequently.

6. Transfer to a plate that has paper towels for them to drain on.

7. Put your rack eight inches from heat when turned on broil. Cook your casserole with it covered until it's heated through and slightly bubbly. This should take about ten minutes, and then cook uncovered until golden brown. This will take less than a minute.

8. Sprinkle your shallots over top right before serving.

Apples & Cornbread

If you're looking for a country side dish to your perfect country Christmas, then you're in for a treat! Though, if you don't have a cast iron skillet, you can finish this in a baking dish. A glass one that's 8x8 is recommended.

Serves: 6-8

Time: 1 Hour

Ingredients:

- 1 Medium Yellow Onion, Sliced Thin
- ¾ Cup + 2 Tablespoons Butter, Unsalted
- 1 Teaspoon Sea Salt + More
- 2 Medium Red Apples, Sliced Thin
- 5 Tablespoons White Sugar, Divided
- 3 Teaspoon Thyme Leaves, Fresh & Divided
- 1 ½ Cups Cornmeal
- 1 Cup All Purpose Flour

- 1 Tablespoon Baking Powder
- 1 ½ Cups Buttermilk
- 2 Large Eggs

Directions:

1. Start by heating your oven to 400, and then melt your butter in your cast iron skillet using medium-high heat. Pour all but two tablespoons of butter into a melted bow, setting the bowl aside.
2. Add in your onion to your butter in the skillet, seasoning with salt and pepper. Make sure that you remember to stir occasionally, cooking until your onion begins to soften and turn brown, which will take about four minutes.
3. Add in your apples, two tablespoons of your sugar, and two teaspoons of thyme and coo until the apples are soft. Stir often, but this will take about four minutes. Transfer your onions into a medium bowl, reserving the skillet.
4. Whisk in your flour, cornmeal, baking powder, a teaspoon of salt, and your remaining three tablespoons of sugar into a large bowl.
5. Whisk your eggs, buttermilk, and three quarter cups of your melted butter until smooth, making sure that no lumps remain.
6. Fold in half of your onion mixture, and then put the mixture into your reserved skillet. Top with your remaining onion mix, and then add your remaining teaspoon of thyme.
7. Bake your cornbread until golden brown, and your fork inserted in the center should come out clean when it's done. It'll take about thirty to forty minutes, and let it cool before serving.

Potato & Leek Gratin

This potato and leek gratin even has celery in it, but don't let the mild ingredients fool you. It certainly doesn't have a mild flavor!

Serves: 8-10

Time: 1 Hour 40 Minutes

Ingredients:

- 3 Cups Heavy Cream
- 1 Spring Thyme + 3 Teaspoons Fresh Thyme Leaves, Divided

- 2 Garlic Cloves, Peeled
- 2 lbs Russet Potatoes, Peeled & Sliced Thin Crosswise
- Sea Salt to Taste
- 3 Leeks, Only using the White and Pale Green Parts, Halved Lengthwise and Sliced Thin Crosswise
- 2 Tablespoons Unsalted Butter, Divided
- 2 Cups Grated Gruyere
- Black Pepper to Taste
- 1 lb Celery Root, Peeled & Sliced Thin Crosswise

Directions:

1. Start by heating your oven to 350, and then heat your thyme sprig, garlic and cream in a medium saucepan. Bubbles should begin to form around the edges before removing from heat. Set it aside, letting it steep.
2. Melt a tablespoon of butter over medium heat in your skilled before adding leeks. Season with salt and then cook until tender, stirring often. Do not let them brown, but it will take about ten minutes. Transfer to a small bowl and set it aside.
3. Butter a three quart dish with your remaining tablespoon of butter. Layer a third of your potato slices and a third of your celery slices evenly at the bottom of your baking dish. Cover with a third of your leeks and a third of your Gruyere. Sprinkle with a teaspoon of thyme leaves, salt and pepper. Repeat the layers twice, and then strain your cream mixture and pour it over your vegetables.
4. Set the gratin dish on a rimmed baking sheet, covering with foil tightly.
5. Bake for an hour, and then remove the foil. Continue to bake until its golden brown and your sauce begins to bubble. This will take about twenty-five to thirty minutes.

Cheddar Biscuits

Sometimes you just want more cheese in your meal, and here's this wonderful recipe to help you add that cheesy goodness you're missing!

Yields: 12-16

Time: 35 Minutes

Ingredients:

- ½ Teaspoon Cream of Tartar
- ½ Teaspoon Cayenne Pepper
- 1 Teaspoon Sea Salt, Fine
- 1 Cup Sharp Cheddar, Grated
- 2/3 Cup Whole Milk
- 8 Tablespoons Butter, Unsalted
- 1 Tablespoon White Sugar
- 2 Cups All Purpose Flour
- 4 Teaspoons Baking Powder

Directions:

1. Start by turning your oven to 425, and then combine your baking powder, salt, flour, cream of tartar, sugar and cayenne together in a bowl.
2. Cut your butter into pieces, and then work it with your fingers until it's crumbly and coarse before stirring in your cheese.
3. Make a well in the center of your flour mixture before pouring your milk in, and stir with a fork until dough forms. Do not overmix this, and then lightly flour a surface to knead it on. Knead it gently for ten to twelve minutes.
4. Pat your dough in circles about ½ inch thick, and then cut out biscuits that are about two inches round. Do not twist your cutter.
5. Transfer these discus onto a buttered baking sheet, baking until golden brown. This should take twelve to fifteen minutes.

Chapter 4: Traditional Christmas Treats

In this chapter you'll find various Christmas treats that you can use to impress your guests or just delight your taste buds. Some are more traditional than others, and you'll find that they're from various regions. Some old American classics, English traditions, Italian favorites, Irish delights, and German treats are included.

Holiday Fruitcake

It's best to start with a common holiday favorite by many. You either love it or hate it, but it usually makes a good gift for someone on your list either way. Here's a traditional fruit cake recipe that is sure to delight anyone who enjoys this traditional treat.

Yields: 1 Cake

Time: 2 Hours 20 Minutes

Ingredients:

- 1 Cup White Sugar
- 5 Large Eggs
- 1 lb Walnut Halves
- 3 Cups Dried Candied Pineapple
- 1 ½ Cups Whole Green Candied Cherries
- 1 ½ Cups Whole Red Candied Cherries
- 4 Tablespoons Pure Vanilla Extract
- 1 Cup Shortening
- 10 Ounces Golden Raisins
- 3 Cups All Purpose Flour
- 3 Teaspoons Baking Powder
- 1 Teaspoon Sea Salt, Fine

Directions:

1. Start by heating your oven to 300, and then combine your fruits and nuts.

2. In a different bowl, cream your shortening and sugar together until it forms a light and fluffy mix. Beat in your vanilla and eggs before combining your salt, baking powder and flour together and adding it into your creamed mix. Make sure to mix well, and pour over your fruit and nuts. Stir to coat.
3. Grease and flour a ten inch tube pan, and then pour your mix in.
4. Bake until a toothpick comes out clean, which should take about 2 hours. Let it cool for ten minutes before removing it from the pan to cool.

Traditional Figgy Pudding

This is a traditional Christmas treat that many people have forgotten to make, but it'll give your country Christmas the perfect dessert.

Serves: 4

Time: 1 Hour 30 Minutes

Ingredients:

- ½ Cup Dried Figs, Chopped
- 1 ½ Cups Dried & Pitted Dates, Chopped
- 3 ½ Ounces Butter, Softened (7 Tablespoons)
- 2 ½ Cups Self-Rising Flour
- 2 ½ Ounces Dark Chocolate, Grated
- Butter to Coat your Ramekins
- 2 Medium Eggs
- 1 Cup Fine Sugar

- 1 Teaspoon Baking Soda
- 2 Cups Water
- Whipped Cream for Garnish

For Sauce:

- 2 Cups Dark Brown Sugar
- 14 Tablespoons Butter
- 2 Cups Heavy Cream
- Fresh Figs, Quartered for Garnish
- Vanilla Ice Cream (Optional)

Directions:

1. Start by heating your oven to 350.
2. Add in your dried figs, water and dates in a saucepan, bringing it to boil over medium heat.
3. Remove them from pan and then stir in your baking soda, letting it cool for five minutes. Pour it into your blender, pureeing.
4. Mix your sugar and butter together to cream, and then add in your eggs, beating well. Fold in your flour and then add in your date mixture. Fold in your chocolate.
5. Butter your ramekins, and pour the mixture in it. It should be filled halfway or slightly under before baking for twenty to twenty-five minutes.
6. To prepare your sauce, stir in your sugar, cream and butter. Simmer until your sugar dissolves over low heat, and then bring it to a boil. Reduce the heat to a simmer for about five minutes, adding in your butter and mixing well.
7. Remove your ramekins from the oven, letting them stand for ten minutes.
8. Pour your sauce over them, and then top with your vanilla ice cream and figs.

Classic Panettone

This is a classic Italian treat which is made in coffee cans, but don't let that fool you. It's still delicious and with no coffee flavor!

Yields: 2 Loaves

Time: 1 Hour 40 Minutes

Ingredients:

Marinated Fruit:

- 1/3 Cup Golden Raisins
- 1/3 Cup Apricots, Dried & Chopped
- ¼ Cup Triple Sec (Orange Flavored Liqueur)

- 1/3 Cup Tart Cherries, Dried

Dough:

- ¼ Teaspoon Granulated Sugar
- 1 Package Dry Yeast (2 ¼ Teaspoons)
- 3 ¾ Cup All Purpose Flour, Divided
- 6 Tablespoons Butter, Melted
- ¼ Cup Warm Water
- ¼ Cup Milk, Fat Free
- ¼ Cup Granulated Sugar
- ½ Teaspoon Sea Salt, Fine
- 1 Large Egg
- 1 Large Egg Yolk
- 2 Tablespoons Pine Nuts
- Cooking Spray as Needed
- 1 Teaspoon Butter, Melted
- 2 Teaspoons Granulated Sugar

Directions:

1. You need to stop preparing your marinated fruit, so combine your raisins, apricots, cherries and triple sec in a bowl. Let it stand for an hour, and then drain in a sieve.
2. Reserve the fruit, and then also keep two teaspoons of the liqueur separately.
3. Next, you'll need to start by preparing your dough. Dissolve yeast and then a quarter teaspoon of your sugar in a warm water. Let it stand for five minutes.
4. Lightly spoon your flour into measuring cups, leveling with a knife. Combine ½ cup of flour with your butter, milk, granulated sugar, salt, egg and your egg yolk in a bowl. Beat at a medium speed for about one minute or at least until smooth. Add in your yeast mixture, and then add in a half a cup of flour, beating for another minute.
5. Stir in your marinated fruit, pine nuts and two and a half cups flour. Turn your dough onto a floured surface, and knead until elastic and smooth. This should take about eight minutes.
6. Add your remaining flour a tablespoon at a time, which will help to prevent the dough from sticking to your hands.
7. Place your dough in a large bowl that you've coated with cooking spray, turning to coat the top.

8. Cover and let it rise in a warm area that doesn't have drafts. This should take about one and a half hours. The dough should double in size.
9. Punch your dough down, and then let it rest for five minutes. Divide it in half, shaping each into a ball.
10. Place the balls in two coffee cans that are also coated with cooking spray, and then cover. Let them rise for about an hour.
11. Heat your oven to 375.
12. Uncover your dough, and then place the coffee cans on the bottom rack of your oven.
13. Bake for about thirty minutes, and the loaves should be browned. They should sound hollow when tapped.
14. Remove from the cans, and let it cool on a wire rack.
15. Combine your two teaspoons of reserved liqueur with a teaspoon of butter, brushing it over your loaves and sprinkling with your sugar.

Old-Fashioned Authentic German Stollen (Christmas Bread)

This is a great way to add a traditional German Treat to your Christmas day, and its sure good with a hot cup of coffee or tea.

Serves: 3 stollen loaves.

Time: 4 hours 20 minutes.

Ingredients:

- 1 1/2 cups milk

- 1/2 cup sugar

- 1 1/2 teaspoons salt

- 3/4 cup butter

- 2 ¼ teaspoons or 1 packet of active dry yeast

- 1 tablespoon sugar

- 2 whole eggs

- 2 egg yolks

- 3 cups sifted all-purpose flour

- 1/2 teaspoon ground cardamom seed

- 1/2 cup raisins

- 1/2 cup finely cut citron

- 1/2 cup sliced candied cherries

- about 2 2/3 cups sifted all-purpose flour
- For the Powdered Sugar Icing
- 1 1/2 cups powdered sugar
- enough cream to make a thick paste
- ½ teaspoon of vanilla extract
- ¼ teaspoons of almond extract

Directions:

1. Scald milk. Add sugar, salt and butter. Cool to lukewarm.
   Mix yeast with 1 tablespoon sugar until liquid. Add to lukewarm milk. Stir.

2. Add whole eggs and egg yolks. Beat.

3. Add 3 cups flour. Beat well. Cover.

4. Let rise in warm place about 1 1/2 hour or until doubled.

5. Add cardamom, raisins, citron, cherries and enough flour until dough pulls from side of bowl and is no longer sticky to the touch.

6. Knead on lightly floured surface until smooth and satiny.

7. Place in lightly greased bowl. Cover. Let rise about 1 1/2 hours or until doubled in bulk.

8. Divide dough into thirds. Use 1/3 for each stollen.

9. Roll on floured canvas into and 8x10 inch oval. Spread with melted butter. Press down center, fold over lengthwise.

10. Place in shallow greased baking pans or on greased cooky sheets. Brush with melted butter.

11. Let rise about 45 minutes or until doubled in bulk.

12. Bake at 350 degrees about 30 minutes.

13.   Frost with Powdered Sugar Icing. Decorate with cherries citron and blanched almonds.

Salted Caramel Pears

If you're looking for a country Christmas, then sometimes a simple dessert is all that it's take. With this caramel recipe, you can use pears or apples, but pears are much more traditional for Christmas.

Serves: 6

Time: 30 Minutes

Ingredients:

- 1/3 Cup Heavy Cream
- 1 Tablespoons Butter
- 6 Pears
- 1 Cup White Sugar
- Flakey Sea Salt

Directions:

1. Heat your sugar over medium heat in a small saucepan, and then stir your sugar occasionally until it dissolves.
2. Cook on high heat until it turns an amber color, and then stir in your heavy cream until smooth.
3. Stir in your butter, and then dip your pears one at a time into the caramel.
4. Sprinkle with flaky sea salt as desired.

Blood Orange Tiramisu

Tiramisu is a classic Italian dessert, and oranges are commonly added to many Christmas recipes. This is a twist on a classic that's sure to taste great.

Serves: 16-20

Time: 11+ Hours

Ingredients:

- 1 ½ Tablespoons Blood Orange Zest
- ¾ Cup Sugar
- 4 Large Eggs, Room Temperature & Separated
- 1 lb Mascarpone Cheese, Room Temperature
- ¼ Teaspoon Sea Salt, Fine
- 4 Tablespoons Grand Marnier
- 40 Ladyfinger Cookies, 4x1 Inch
- Chocolate Shavings
- 1/3 Cup Dark Cocoa Powder, Unsweetened
- 6 Blood Oranges, Juiced (Roughly 2 Cups)

Directions:

1. Beat your egg yolks and sugar together over medium-high heat until it starts to thicken and is light. This will take from three to six minutes, and then switch to a paddle attachment to add in your mascarpone cheese, beating until it's mixed well.
2. Add in your zest and then add two tablespoons of grand Marnier, and then beat until its combined well. Transfer into a large bowl.
3. Place your egg whites in a different bowl and whisk. Sprinkle your salt over the egg whites, beating on medium-high speed with the whisk attachment until soft peaks form, which will take four to five minutes.
4. Add in half of your egg whites to your egg yolk mix, and gently fold them together until they're almost completely mixed.
5. Add your remaining egg whites, gently folding them to completely incorporate it into your mixture.
6. Stir your blood orange juice with the rest of your grand Marnier.
7. You'll need to work quickly by dipping twenty of your lady fingers in the juice mixture, soaking the cookie from top to bottom. Then arrange them to cover the bottom of your pan. It should be 9x13 inches. Dollop half of your mascarpone mixture over your ladyfingers, spreading it in an even layer.
8. Sift half of your cocoa powder on top of this layer, and then dip your next twenty lady fingers in the juice, arranging them over the mascarpone layer. Cover the ladyfingers with the rest of your mascarpone mix, spreading it into an even layer. Sift the rest of your cocoa powder on top.
9. Cover with plastic wrap, and then refrigerate for about five hours or overnight. Most people prefer it if it's been chilled for about ten hours more. Sprinkle with chocolate shavings before serving.

Sugared Cranberries

These spiced delights are unusual to be served in this day and age, but they're a treat that shouldn't be forgotten.

Yields: 2 Cups

Time: 2 Hours 20 Minutes

Ingredients:

Simple Syrup:

- ¾ Cup Granulated Sugar
- 2 Cinnamon Sticks
- 2 Whole Star Anise
- ¾ Cup Water
- ½ Teaspoon Whole Allspice

Cranberries:

- ¾ Cup Granulated Sugar
- 2 Cups Cranberries, Fresh

Directions:

1. You'll need to start by making your syrup by adding your star anise, allspice, cinnamon sticks, water and sugar together in a saucepan. Cook over medium-high heat, cooking while stirring frequently until your sugar is completely dissolved.
2. Let it come to a boil and then turn the heat down, letting it simmer for five minutes. Remove from heat.
3. Let it cool to room temperature, and then remove your allspice, star anise and cinnamon sticks.
4. Line a baking sheet with foil and then add your cranberries into your saucepan with your cooled simple syrup.
5. Stir to coat it, and then shake off the excess syrup by pulling them out with a slotted spoon. Transfer to your pan, and spread in an even layer. Let it dry for one hour.
6. Add your three quarter cups of sugar in a bowl, and then roll your cranberries in the sugar in batches. Let it dry for one to two hours, and then store in an airtight container. Refrigerate for up to a week.

Chocolate Pretzels

Chocolate covered candies are often used as gifts for Christmas or just a treat to enjoy, so here's an easy recipe to use.

Yields: 1-2 Cups

Time: 15-25 Minutes

Ingredients:

- 1 Cup White Chocolate Chips
- 1 Teaspoon Vegetable Oil
- Red Candy Melts
- Pretzels

Directions:

1. Melt your white chocolate in intervals of thirty seconds, and then add your vegetable oil, stirring it in.
2. The chocolate should become smooth, and dip in your pretzels, laying them out in a single layer. Try to cover them.
3. Melt your red candy melts. Make sure to melt in thirty second intervals, and then put them in an icing pipe to drizzle over as desired.

Gingerbread

Gingerbread is traditionally German for Christmas, but similar recipes actually date back to Egypt. Still, it's a great recipe to try even if you don't want to build a gingerbread house.

Serves: 25-32

Time: 45 Minutes

Ingredients:

- ½ Cup Butter, Softened
- 4 Medium Eggs
- 1 Cup Granulated Sugar
- 2 Tablespoons Cocoa Powder
- 1 Tablespoon Lebkuchen Spice blend
- 1 Cup Whole Milk
- 1 ½ Teaspoons Baking Powder
- ½ Cup Candied Lemon Peeled, Chopped
- 1 Tablespoon Rum (or Orange Liqueur)
- 1 ¾ Cups Almonds, Ground

Glaze:

- ½ Cup Granulated Sugar
- ¼ Cup Water
- 1-2 Tablespoons Rum (Or Liqueur)
- ½ Cup Powdered Sugar
- ½ Teaspoons Vanilla Extract, Pure

Spices:

- 2 Tablespoons Ground Cinnamon
- 2 Teaspoons Ground Cloves
- ½ Teaspoons Ground Allspice
- ¼ Teaspoon Ground Nutmeg
- ½ Teaspoon Ground Cardamom
- ½ Teaspoon Ground Coriander
- ½ Teaspoon Ground Ginger
- ½ Teaspoon Ground Anise Seed

Extras:

- ½ Cup Raisins, Soaked in Rum & Chopped
- ¼ Cup Coconut, Shredded

Directions:

1. Mix your spices and then divide out what you need for this recipe.
2. Cream your eggs, butter and sugar until fluffy and light.
3. Mix in your spices, cocoa powder, baking powder, flour and milk.
4. Fold in your lemon peel, nuts and then stir in your rum. Stir in your raisins and coconut if you choose to use them.
5. Draw three inch circles on parchment paper, and then cut them with a biscuit cutter.
6. Drop three tablespoons of cookie dough on each.
7. Fill out each circle with the back of your spoon. You should slightly mound the dough towards the center.
8. Turn your oven to 375, and then bake to fifteen to twenty minutes. Turn it down to 350 if you find your cookies browning too quickly.
9. Let them cool, and while they're warm you'll want to make your glaze.
10. Place your sugar and water in a saucepan and bring it to a boil. Boil for a few minutes before adding your liqueur or rum as well as your vanilla. Sift in your powdered sugar over your hot syrup and then stir.

11.   Use a brush to brush this glaze over your cookies and then let
   dry.

CHRISTMAS IN ALASKA

Baked Alaska

This is an old fashioned American recipe that is sure to impress and taste great.

Yields: 1 Cake

Time: 3+ Hours

Ingredients:

- 6 Tablespoons Granulated Sugar
- 3 Large Egg Whites, Room Temperature
- 1 Teaspoon Vanilla Extract, Pure
- Swiss Meringue
- 3 Large Egg Yolks
- Pinch Sea Salt, Fine
- 3 Ounces Bittersweet Chocolate, Melted & Cooled
- 1 ½ Pints Cherry Ice Cream, Softened Slightly (Or Berry Sorbet)
- Vegetable Oil Cooking Spray as Needed

Directions:

1. Start by heating your oven to 350, and then line an eight inch round pan with parchment paper. Spray it down with cooking spray.
2. Combine three tablespoons of your sugar and egg yolks in a bowl, and whisk with a whisk attachment on medium speed. It should be thick, and pale yellow. It'll take about fifteen minutes, and then add in your vanilla. Fold in your melted chocolate, making sure to combine.
3. Combine your egg whites and a pinch of salt, whipping on medium speed until it becomes frothy. Add in the rest of your sugar, beating until it gets stiff.
4. Fold in your egg whites into the chocolate mixture, and then pour in the cake pan. Bake until the top is dull, which will take about twenty minutes.
5. Remove from the oven, letting it cool.
6. Spray a five cup bowl, metal is better, and then line with plastic wrap.
7. Pack your bowl by layering desired ice cream or sorbet, and then firmly cover the surface with plastic wrap, placing it in the freezer. The

ice cream should become hard in about two hours, but you can leave it up to twenty-four hours.

8. Place your cake on a baking sheet lined with parchment paper, and then remove your ice cream from the freezer.
9. Invert the bowl over your cake, and then keep the ice cream covered in plastic wrap on top. Return this ice cream cake to your freezer.
10. Heat your over to 500, and then fill a pastry bag with meringue. Pipe into your ice cream as decoratively as you like, and swirl it with a spatula.
11. Make sure your plastic is off! Place in the oven and bake until meringue starts to brown which will take one to two minutes. Serve immediately.

Fig Holiday Cake Roll

Fig is a common and traditional fruit that's used in many Christmas dishes, and a holiday roll is the perfect but simple dessert to make and enjoy.

Yields: 1 Cake

Time: 5+ Hours

Ingredients:

Cake:

- 8 Tablespoons Unsalted Butter, Melted & Cooled + More for Pan & Foil
- 1 lb Soft Dried Figs, Quartered & Stems Removed
- ¼ Cup Currants, Dried
- 1 ½ Cups Whole Milk
- ¾ Cup Light Brown Sugar, Packed
- 1 ½ Cups All Purpose Flour
- 2 ½ Teaspoons Baking Powder
- 1 Teaspoon Ground Cinnamon
- ½ Teaspoon Nutmeg, Freshly Grated
- ¼ Teaspoon Ground Cloves
- ¼ Teaspoon Ground Ginger
- 3 Slices White Bread
- ½ Teaspoon Sea Salt, Fine
- 4 Large Eggs

- 2 Tablespoons Crystalized Ginger (Optional)
- 2 Tablespoons Candied Kumquats, Chopped (Optional)

Filling & Garnish:

- 2 lbs Mascarpone Cheese
- ½ Cup Heavy Cream
- Red Currants for Garnish
- Raspberry Coulis
- Candied Kumquats for Garnish
- ½ Cup Confectioner's Sugar

Directions:

1. Start by heating your oven to 350.
2. To make the cake, butter a jelly roll pan that's 18x12 inches.
3. Line it with parchment paper and then butter the parchment paper.
4. Place your dried currants, milk, and figs in saucepan, bringing it to simmer. Use medium heat, and cook until the liquid is absorbed which will take eight to ten minutes.
5. Remove it from heat, and then place the mix in a food processor, process until it becomes a thick paste. It shouldn't be completely smooth, and then set it aside.
6. Sift your brown sugar, flour, cinnamon, baking powder, ginger, cloves, salt and nutmeg in a bowl, setting it aside.
7. Tear your bread into small pieces and then place in a food processor, pulsing until your crumbs form. Pulse ten times, which should yield one and a half cups breadcrumbs.
8. Place your eggs in a bowl, using an electric mixer with a paddle attachment beat on high. It should become frothy, and then reserve the fig mixture, kumquats, ginger, breadcrumbs and melted butter, mixing it all in. turn your mixer to low, and add in your four mix, mixing until combined well.
9. Bring three cups of water to a boil in a medium saucepan, and then spread your batter as evenly as you can in a prepared pan. Cover the pan loosely with your buttered foil, and then place in the middle rack of your oven. Another baking pan that you fill with boiling water should be beneath your cake rack. Bake until your cake is springy, and a fork should come out clean. This will take about forty minutes, and then rotate it once halfway through your baking time.
10. Remove it from the oven, and let it cool on a cooling rack for ten minutes.

11. Lay a kitchen towel and a sheet pan over your cake, inverting your cake onto the towel.
12. Allow it to cool for ten minutes, and then curl the cake using your towel without applying too much pressure. Allow it to stay wrapped in your towel for ten minutes, unroll and let cool at room temperature.
13. There are going to be some breaks in the cake, but now you'll need to start making your filling. Combine your cream, mascarpone, and confectioner's sugar in a bowl, folding until it's completely mixed and smooth.
14. Place this mix in the fridge until you're ready for it. It's going to be easier to roll your cake if this mix is cold, and then spread the chilled ix over your unrolled cake.
15. Roll your cake up again, and leave the cake ends exposed. Secure with cloth pins and chill your rolled cake for a minimum of four hours. Many people leave it overnight, and then it should be left to stand for thirty minutes before serving.
16. Trim the ends off the cake before serving, and garnish with raspberry coulis, candied kumquats and red currants if desired.

Christmas Fruit Tart

Fruit tarts are an English favorite, but this Christmas fruit tart uses winter fruits to make a perfect holiday blend.

Serves: 8

Time: 2 Hours 20 Minutes

Ingredients:

- Pie Dough
- ¼ Teaspoon Sea Salt, Fine
- ½ Teaspoon Ground Allspice
- 1 Cup All Purpose Flour + Some For Dusting
- ½ Teaspoon Ground Cinnamon
- 1 Teaspoon Ground Ginger
- ½ Teaspoon Nutmeg, Freshly Grated
- ¼ Cup Currants
- ½ Cups + 2 Tablespoons Dark Brown Sugar

- ¼ Cup Golden Raisins
- ¼ Cup Citron
- ¼ Cup Candied Orange Peel, Chopped in ¼ Inch Pieces
- 1 Cup Blanched Almonds, Finely Chopped & Toasted
- Zest of 1 Lemon, Finely Grated
- 3 Tablespoons Brandy
- 2 Large Eggs
- ¼ Cup Molasses, Unsulfured
- 2 Tablespoons Lemon Juice, Fresh

Directions:

1. Lightly flour a surface to work on, and roll out ¾ of your pie dough to fit in a rectangular 13x4 inch tart pan. It should be 1/8 inch thick. Place it in a pastry pan, and then gently press down with your fingers and along the rim trim the pastry as needed, and then refrigerate with your remaining dough while you make your filling.
2. Sift your spices, flour and salt into a bowl before adding your citron, dried fruit, orange peel, sugar, almonds, zest and juice together.
3. Stir in your molasses, one beaten egg and brandy. Pack this into your pastry lined tin.
4. Roll out the remaining dough to 1/8 inch thickness on your floured surface. Moisten the edges with water, and then roll your dough over the filling. Seal well, trimming the excess dough off and chill for an hour.
5. Heat your oven to 325, and then make three slits in it to serve as air vents. Whisk the remaining egg with a tablespoon of water in a bowl. Brush your tart with this egg wash, and place it in the oven. Bake until its golden brown and flaky. It should take about one hour and forty minutes, and let it cool on a rack at room temperature before slicing to serve.

Old Fashion Divinity

This divinity is just like your mother used to make, and it's sure to bring back good memories. If you're one of those unlucky few that never got to try this white Christmas treat, then this is your chance to try a traditional Christmas recipe to pass down for generations to come.

Yields: 40+

Time: 35 Minutes

Ingredients:

- 4 Cups Granulated Sugar
- 1 Cup Light Corn Syrup
- 1 Cup Cold Water
- 1 Teaspoon Vanilla Extract, Pure
- 3 Egg Whites
- 1 Cup Pecans

Directions:

1. Prepare two to three baking sheets by placing wax paper over them.
2. Take a heavy bottomed saucepan and place it over medium heat with your water, corn syrup and sugar in it. Stir only until your sugar dissolves. Don't stir after this point. Cook until the temperature reaches 255 using a candy thermometer to check. This should bring it to a hard ball stage.
3. While this is happening, beat your egg whites in a stand mixture until stiff. Once your candy has reached 255, carefully pour a slow and steady stream of the syrup into your egg whites. Beat constantly at high speed, adding in your vanilla and beating until the mixture holds its shape easily. This will roughly take five minutes, and then add pecans at the end, folding them in with a spoon.
4. Spray 2 spoons with oil to keep your divinity form sticking. Place the divinity onto wax paper. When placing on the baking sheet, try to mimic the look of soft serve ice cream, and if the candy becomes too stiff to swirl properly you can add a few drops of hot water to loosen. You'll need to work quickly, and it's usually best to get someone to help you twirl the ends if you want to get them all before they're too hard to swirl.

Classic Chocolate Fudge

This fudge recipe is perfect for Christmas, and it packs well to make Christmas gifts too.

Yields: 60

Time: 25-35 Minutes

Ingredients:

- 2 Cups White Sugar
- ½ Cup Cocoa
- 1 Cup Whole Milk
- 1 Teaspoon Vanilla Extract, Pure
- 4 Tablespoons Butter

Directions:

1. Start by greasing an eight by eight inch pan and set it aside.
2. Combine your milk, sugar and cocoa in a saucepan. Stir and bring it to a boil, making sure to continue stirring constantly. Reduce the heat, letting it simmer and don't stir again.
3. Place your candy thermometer in the pan, cooking until it reaches 238 degrees.
4. When you drop a piece of the mix in cold water it should form a soft ball. You'll want to check to make sure it has the right consistency, so make sure it flattens when pressed between your two fingers.
5. Remove from heat, and then add your butter as well as your vanilla extract. Beat with a wooden spoon, and the fudge should lose its sheen. Don't under beat.
6. Pour into a pan, letting it cool before cutting into sixty squares.

Cranberry & Pecan Shortbread

Shortbread is a common English dessert, and this shortbread recipe has been spiced up to make it perfect for your winter holiday festivities.

Serves: 8-10

Time: 1 Hour 40 Minutes

Ingredients:

- ½ Teaspoon Shortening
- 1 Cup Powdered Sugar
- ¾ Cup Toasted Pecan Halves, Divided
- ½ Teaspoon Orange Zest
- ½ Cup Sweetened Cranberries, Dried
- 10 Tablespoons Unsalted Butter, Melted
- Vegetable Cooking Spray
- ¼ Teaspoon Sea Salt, Fine
- 1 Cup All Purpose Flour
- ¼ Cup Semi-Sweet Chocolate Morsels

Directions:

1. Start by heating your oven to 325. Process one half a cup of pecans in your food processor, making sure it's finely ground. Add your powdered sugar, unsalted butter, cranberries, orange zest, and salt together. Pulse until your cranberries are chopped coarsely. Add in your flour, and pulse until it's mixed well.
2. Spread your dough over a nine inch tart pan that's been lightly greased. This pan is best if you have a removable bottom, and press the rest of your pecans into the dough.
3. Bake at 325 for thirty to thirty-five minutes, making sure that your edges turn out golden.
4. Remove the sides of your pan, and cut your shortbread into eight to ten wedges, transferring the wedges onto a parchment lined baking sheet.
5. Bake for ten minutes or until firm, and then let cool.

6. Microwave your chocolate on high for one minute or until smooth. After your first minute stir and microwave for thirty second intervals until smooth.
7. Drizzle over your cookies once cool and let stand until the chocolate is set. This will take about ten minutes.

Thumbprint Cookies

This is another traditional American favorite, and you'll find that it can be easily personalized. You can add any jam or preserve you want to make your own unique twist on this recipe.

Serves: 12

Time: 30 Minutes

Ingredients:

- ½ Cup Butter, Softened
- 1 Cup All Purpose Flour
- 1 Medium Egg
- ¼ Teaspoon Sea Salt, Fine
- 2/3 Cup Raspberry Fruit Jam
- ¼ Cup Walnuts, Chopped Fine
- ½ Teaspoon Vanilla Extract, Pure
- ¼ Cup Light Brown Sugar, Packed

Directions:

1. Start by heating your oven to 300, and then grease your cookie sheet.
2. Start by separating your egg and reserve the egg white. Cream your egg yolk, sugar, and butter together.
3. Add in your flour, salt and vanilla, making sure to mix well.
4. Form your dough into balls, rolling in your egg white and then roll these balls into your walnuts.
5. Place on your cookie sheet about two inches away from each other and bake for five minutes.
6. Remove your cookies from the oven, and dent each cookie with your thumb.
7. Place a dollop of raspberry preserves in each thumbprint, baking for eight more minutes.

Bread Pudding & Vanilla Sauce

Bread pudding is an old English recipe that came to America quickly, and it's traditional and tasty too.

Serves: 6-8

Time: 50 Minutes

Ingredients:

- ¼ Cup Butter, Melted
- 1 ½ Cups Granulated Sugar
- 3 Large Eggs, Beaten Lightly
- ½ Teaspoon Ground Nutmeg
- 2 Tablespoons Light Brown Sugar
- 2 ¾ Cup Whipping Cream
- 4 Cups French Bread, Cubed
- ¾ Cup Raisins

Vanilla Sauce:

- ½ Cup Granulated Sugar
- ¼ Teaspoon Ground Nutmeg

- 1 Tablespoon All Purpose Flour
- 3 Tablespoons Light Brown Sugar
- 1 Large Egg
- 1 ¼ Cup Whipping Cream
- 2 Tablespoons Butter
- 1 Tablespoon Vanilla Extract, Pure

Directions:

1. Start by combining your eggs, sugar, brown sugar and nutmeg to make your bread pudding. Stir in your butter and whipping cream.
2. Gently mix in your raisins and bread, and then pour it into a two quart baking dish.
3. Bake at 375 for fifty to fifty-five minutes, making sure it's covered in foil after it's cooked for a half hour.
4. Let pudding stand for ten minutes, and while doing this make your vanilla sauce.
5. Whisk your sugar, light brown sugar, nutmeg, flour, egg, whipping cream and butter together in a saucepan. Cook over medium heat, and continue to whisk constantly.
6. Do this for ten to twelve minutes until thickened, and once you remove it from heat stir in our vanilla.
7. It's best to serve this warm.

Traditional Struffoli

This is a traditional Italian Christmas recipe, and it originates from Naples. This is a crispy dough with citrus flavor.

Serves: 10

Time: 40 Minutes

Ingredients:

- 1 Cup All Purpose Flour
- 1 Lemon Zest
- 1 Orange Zest
- 1 ½ Tablespoons White Sugar
- ¼ Tablespoons Sea Salt, Fine
- 2 Ounces Butter, Unsalted
- ¼ Tablespoon Baking Powder
- 1/3 Tablespoon Vanilla Extract, Pure
- Vegetable Oil for Frying
- 2 Egg Medium
- ½ Cup Honey, Raw
- ½ Tablespoons Lemon Juice, Fresh
- ¼ Cup White Sugar
- Candied Fruits (Optional)
- Confectioner's Sugar (Optional)

- ½ Tablespoons Rum or Brandy

Directions:

1. Mix your lemon, orange zest, flour, sugar, salt and baking powder together.
2. Mix your dry ingredients with your butter in a food processor, and blend until all of the lumps in your butter are almost gone, and it should resemble a coarse meal.
3. Slowly add eggs as well as vanilla extract, blending until your dough becomes a large ball.
4. Cover the dough with saran wrap and wrap, keeping it in your fridge for about a half hour.
5. Roll your dough into thick cords about a quarter inch thick. You'll need to cut the dough into about half inch pieces and then roll them in small balls. They should be about the size of a hazelnut.
6. Lightly dust these with flour, but make sure not to put too much flour on them either.
7. Take a saucepan with oil in it, heating it over medium heat. Once it hits 375 you can fry the dough in batches. It should take about two to three minutes on each batch, and they should turn a light golden brown.
8. Put them on a plate with paper towels to let them drain.
9. You'll want to combine your rum or brandy, lemon juice, extra sugar and honey in a saucepan over medium heat. Cook the mixture, stirring until your sugar is completely dissolved.
10. Turn off the heat, and then add your fried dough balls, stirring them carefully. You want to make sure you don't damage your dough.
11. Once they're covered, place them on a serving platter and set it to the side. Pour some of the remaining honey mix on top, and then sprinkle with confectioner's sugar or candied fruit.

Christmas in Italy

Piedmontese Hazelnut Cake

This is another traditional Italian Christmas cake, and it's easy to make with a relatively short ingredient list. Of course, you have to enjoy hazelnut to enjoy this cake.

Yields: 1 Cake

Time: 40 Minutes

Ingredients:

- 1 ¼ Cup Granulated Sugar
- Vegetable Oil to Grease the Pan
- 1 ½ Cups Hazelnuts, Lightly Toasted & Skins Removed
- 4 Large Egg Whites, Room Temperature
- 4 Large Egg Yolks, Room Temperature
- ¼ Teaspoon Sea Salt, Fine
- Confectioner's Sugar for Dusting
- Berries to Garnish (Optional)

Directions:

1. Adjust your oven rack to the center position before turning it to 350, and then grease a nine inch spring-form pan. Make sure that it's greased well.
2. Combine your hazelnuts with a quarter cup of your white sugar in a food processor, and process until your hazelnuts are finely ground.
3. Place your egg whites in the bowl along with a quarter cup of sugar and a pinch of salt. Beat on high until your egg whites are glossy, and they should form soft peaks. Set this bowl aside.
4. Combine your egg yolks and three quarters cup of sugar in another bowl, beating on high. You'll need to stop quite a few times to scrape the sides down, continuing to beat until the mix becomes pale yellow and thick.
5. Use a spatula to add in your hazelnuts to your egg yolks, and then spoon a quarter of your beaten egg whites into your hazelnut batter. Stir to lighten, and then fold the remaining egg whites in the mix. You should work from the bottom of the bowl and turn it upward, and you shouldn't be able to see any streaks of white.

6. Turn your batter into your pan, smoothing the top out. Place in your oven.
7. As it bakes, it will rise. Consistent heat is important so make sure that you don't open the oven to check on it. After twenty minutes, quickly open the oven and press gently at the center of the cake. If the top of the cake is golden and the center firm, then remove it from your oven and let cool on a wire rack. If it isn't, then bake for an additional five minutes.
8. Allow your cake to cool until it's just barely warm. Run a knife around the edges of your pan, and remove and put on a platter. Dust with confectioner's sugar and add your berries to garnish before serving.

Classic Christmas Pudding

Most people don't think of Christmas pudding when they hear pudding. Traditionally, you'll find that it has a different texture than most people are used to. This is an English recipe that many Americans still enjoy. This recipe uses mixed spice, which is not allspice.

Serves: 6-8

Time: 8 Hours 45 Minutes

Ingredients:

- 1 lb Mixed Dried Fruit
- 1 Ounce Candied Peel, Chopped Fine
- 1 Small Apple, Peeled, Cored & Finely Chopped
- 1 Tablespoon Orange Zest
- 1 Tablespoon Lemon Zest
- 4 Tablespoons Brandy + Plus Some for Soaking
- 1 Tablespoon Lemon Juice, Fresh
- 2 Tablespoons Orange Juice, Fresh
- 2 Ounces Self-Rising Flour, Sifted

- 1 Teaspoon Mixed Spice, Ground
- ½ Teaspoon Cinnamon, Ground
- 4 Ounces Suet (Vegetarian or Beef, Shredded)
- 14 Ounces Brown Sugar, Dark & Soft
- 4 Ounces Bread Crumbs, White & Fresh
- 1 Ounces Almond, Whole, Shelled & Roughly Chopped
- 2 Large Eggs

Mixed Spice:

- 1 Tablespoon Ground Cinnamon
- 2 Teaspoons Ground Mace
- 1 Tablespoon Ground Nutmeg
- 1 Teaspoon Ground Cloves
- 1 Teaspoon Ground Coriander
- 1 Tablespoons Ground Allspice
- 1 Teaspoon Ground Ginger

Directions:

1. Mix all of your mixed spice ingredients together and then pull out the amount you need for this recipe. Store the rest in an airtight container.
2. Lightly butter a two and a half pudding basin.
3. Place your apple, orange juice, lemon juice, dried fruits and candied peel in a mixing bowl. Add in your brandy, making sure to stir well.
4. Cover the bowl, and let this marinate for at least a couple of hours. It's best if you leave it overnight.
5. Stir your cinnamon, flour and mixed spice together in a mixing bowl. Add in your suet, sugar, orange zest, lemon zest, nuts, and bread crumbs, stirring again. Make sure it's all mixed well, and then stir in your marinated fruit.
6. Beat your eggs lightly, and then stir it quickly into your dry ingredient mix. It should have a soft consistency once mixed together.
7. Spoon the mixture into your greased pudding basin, and press the mixture down with the back of your spoon. Cover it with a double layer of paper that's greaseproof. Baking parchment will usually work. Put a layer of foil over it, and tie it securely with a string, wrapping it around the basin. Tie it so that it forms a handle so that you can lift the pudding from the steamer.
8. Place your pudding in a steamer over a saucepan that has water simmering in it, and steam this pudding mix for seven hours. The

water level will need to be checked frequently, and it should never boil dry. The pudding will lightly be dark brown in color once it's cooked. It should be dark, sticky and have a sponge like consistency.

9. Remove your pudding from the steamer and let it completely cool.

10. Remove the paper, and prick your pudding with a skewer. You will then want to pour more brandy over it.

11. Cover and store until it's ready to be eaten.

Southern Pecan Pie

If you're looking for a southern country Christmas, it just wouldn't be complete without a pecan pie. This recipe is simple to make and simply delicious to boot!

Yields: 1 Pie

Time: 4 Hours 10 Minutes

Ingredients:

- 4 Large Eggs
- 1 ½ Cups Light Brown Sugar, Firmly Packed
- 1 Tablespoons Powdered Sugar
- 14.1 Ounce Piecrust Package, Refrigerated
- ½ Cup Granulated Sugar
- ½ Cup Pecans, Chopped
- 2 Tablespoons All Purpose Flour
- 2 Tablespoons Whole Milk
- ½ Cup Butter, Melted

- 1 ½ Teaspoons Bourbon
- 1 ½ Cups Pecans, Halved

Directions:

1. Start by heating your oven to 325, and fit your crust into a ten inch cast iron skillet. Sprinkle some powdered sugar over your piecrust.
2. Whisk your eggs in a bowl until it's foamy, and then whisk in your brown sugar, butter, sugar, bourbon, pecans, all-purpose flour, and milk. Pour it into your pie crust and then top with your other pecan halves.
3. Bake for thirty minutes, and reduce the temperature to 300 before baking another half hour.
4. Turn the oven off, and let your pie stand with the door closed for three hours.

Chapter 5: Christmas Jarred Gift Recipes

Sometimes the best gift is something you make yourself, but you want to make sure that you give someone something they'll want or use too. That's where these jarred gift recipes come in handy, and they're the perfect addition to your country Christmas.

Jarred Spiced Butter & Fresh Pound Cake

This is a jarred recipe that goes great with any fresh bread or pound cake, but we'll teach you how to make a quick and easy holiday pancake to go with it. Just make sure that you keep your jar refrigerated before giving it away so that it stays good.

Time: 2 Hours 30 Minutes

Ingredients:

Honey Spread:

- 1 Cup Honey, Raw
- 1 Cup Butter, Softened
- 1 Cup Powdered Sugar
- 2 Teaspoons Ground Cinnamon
- 3 Half Pint Canning Jars

Pound Cake:

- 1 ½ Cups Butter, Softened
- 2 Teaspoons Vanilla Extract, Pure
- 3 Cups All Purpose Flour
- 3 Cups Sugar
- 6 Medium Eggs
- 8 Ounces Cream Cheese, Softened
- ½ Teaspoon Baking Powder
- ¼ Teaspoon Sea Salt, Fine
- 1 Teaspoon Almond Extract

Directions:

1. Start by making your honey spread. You'll want to combine all of your ingredient in a bowl and blend until smooth.
2. Pour into your jars and keep refrigerated until it's time to give them away.
3. Now you'll want to move onto your pound cake. Cream your butter, sugar and cream cheese together until fluffy and light. Add in your eggs one egg at a time, making sure that you beat well each time you add one. Beat in your extracts next.

4. Combine your salt, baking powder and flour before beating it into your creamed mixture.
5. Grease a floured ten inch flute tube pan, and then pour your batter in.
6. Turn your oven to 325, and bake for one hour fifteen minutes to one hour and thirty minutes. When you insert a toothpick it should come out clean. If you're making mini loaves it should take only thirty-five minutes.
7. Let it cool before removing from pan. You'll want to wrap it in paper and tie with twine to give it as a gift with your honey spread.

Jarred Peppermint Brownies

Most everyone loves brownies, but finding a good brownie mix can be hard. That's where this jarred gift comes in handy.

Ingredients:

- 2/3 Cup Cocoa Powder
- 2 Cups White Sugars
- 1 ¼ Cups Flour
- ½ Teaspoon Sea Salt, Fine
- 1 Cup Peppermint Baking Chips

Directions:

1. Layer the ingredients in a mason jar, and add instructions.

Instructions:

- Mix your jar with a cup of butter that's been melted, four medium eggs, two teaspoons of vanilla and bake at 350 for twenty-five minutes to enjoy!

Mocha Cocoa

If you have a chocolate and coffee lover on your Christmas list, then you might want to try this jarred Christmas recipe as a gift option.

Ingredients:

- 1 Cup Cocoa Powder, Unsweetened
- 1 Cup White Sugar
- 1 Cup Powdered Milk
- ½ Cup Espresso Powder
- ½ Cup Bittersweet Chocolate, Chopped
- ½ Teaspoon Sea Salt, Fine

Directions:

1. Just layer your cocoa on the bottom, then your sugar, then espresso. Your next layers should be your powdered milk, salt and chocolate.

Instructions:

1. Mix contents in a large bowl, and for each serving you'll use 1/3 cup of your mix. Place it in a mug and stir in a cup of boiling water. Keep the rest stored in an airtight container.

Rosemary & Mint Sugar Scrub

This isn't a recipe that you should eat even if it's edible. It's a great gift for the more girly-girls on your list. If they like a minty scent and want smooth skin, then this is the right gift for them.

Ingredients:

- 1 Cup Sugar
- ½ Cup Sweet Almond Oil
- 8-10 Drops Rosemary Essential Oil
- 5-8 Drops Mint Essential Oil

Directions:

1. Stir together and store in an airtight jar.

Jasmine Bath Salts

These jarred bath salts are another non-edible gift that can be given and mad easily with this recipe. It's perfect for anyone on your list that wants smooth skin!

Ingredients:

- 1 Cup Epsom Salts
- 1 Tablespoon Baking Soda
- 5 Drops Jasmine Essential Oil
- 1 Drop Red Food Coloring

Directions:

1. Mix together and store in an airtight jar before giving away.

Jarred Cranberry Cookie Mix

This is a great Christmas cookie mix that is fun to make, and it makes a beautiful jarred gift.

Ingredients:

- ½ Teaspoon Sea Salt, Fine
- ½ Cup Rolled Oats
- 1 Cup + 2 Tablespoons All Purpose Flour
- ½ Teaspoon Baking Soda
- 1/2 Cup Cranberries, Dried
- 1/3 Cup White Sugar
- 1/3 Cup Brown Sugar, Packed
- ½ Cup White Chocolate Chips
- ½ Cup Chopped Pecans

Directions:

1. Layer ingredients evenly.

Instructions:

- Heat the oven to 350 and grease a cookie sheet. Beat together a half a cup of softened butter, a teaspoon of vanilla extract and an egg until fluffy. Add your jar mix, and make sure it's mixed well. Bake for eight to ten minutes or until golden brown.

Cinnamon Popcorn

A lot of people love popcorn, but giving popcorn as a gift doesn't have to be boring!

Ingredients:

- ½ Cup Popcorn Kernels
- 2 Tablespoons Granulated Sugar
- 1 Teaspoon Ground Cinnamon
- ½ Teaspoon Ginger, Ground

Directions:

1. Place your kernels in a jar and then mix your seasoning in another packet, tying it to the jar with ribbon.

Instructions:

- Cover the bottom of a pot with oil before placing over medium heat. Add in your kernels and loosely cover for popping. Lower the heat once it starts and shake your pot. Once popped and while it's warm, shake your mixture over it and serve.

Jarred Tropical Tea Soak

If you know someone that loves to pamper themselves, then they'll like this jarred bath soak recipe as their Christmas gift.

Ingredients:

- ½ Cup Cornstarch
- 2 Teaspoons Green Tea with Mango Leaves
- 2 Teaspoons Peach Tea Leaves
- ½ Cup Oatmeal
- 1 Cup Dry Milk

Directions:

1. Grind your oatmeal up and then add all of your ingredients to a food processor. Process before putting into a jar and sealing.

Instructions:

- Add two tablespoons of this mix to a warm bath, and sit back and relax!

Jarred Apple Butter

Sometimes preserves is the best gift that you can give someone, especially if they live a busy lifestyle. This is a simple apple butter spread that anyone is sure to enjoy.

Yield: 4 Pints

Time: 12 Hours

Ingredients:

- ½ Teaspoon Nutmeg, Freshly Grated
- 1 Tablespoon Ground Cinnamon
- 6 ½ lbs Apples, Cored, Peeled & Sliced
- 1 Tablespoon Ground Cinnamon
- ¼ Teaspoon Ground Cloves
- 1 Cup White Sugar
- 1 Cup Light Brown Sugar, Packed Lightly
- ¼ Teaspoon Sea Salt, Fine
- 1 Tablespoon Vanilla Extract, Pure

Directions:

1. Place your apples in a slow cooker, and then get out a bowl.
2. In your bowl combine your sugars, cinnamon, salt, cloves and nutmeg. Pour this mix over your apples.
3. The slow cooker should be on low for ten hours, and you'll want to stir them occasionally. The mix should thicken to a dark brown.
4. Uncover and then stir in your vanilla, and continue to cook on low for another two hours.

5. Use an immersion blender, and puree your apple butter until it's completely smooth.
6. Spoon into jars and store for up to two weeks. Remember to make them right before you give them out, and make sure that you have their expiration date on there! If you can the recipe they'll last even longer.

Spiced Pear Jam

Preserves and jams always make a great gift, but sometimes you want something a little more festive than apple butter. That's where this spiced pear jam comes in handy. It has that holiday feel to the taste, making it a perfect and simple Christmas gift.

Yields: 6 Half Pints

Time: 1 Hour 50 Minutes

Ingredients:

- 8 Cups Pears, Peeled & Chopped (Roughly 5 ½ lbs)
- 4 Cups Granulated Sugar
- ½ Teaspoon Ground Cloves
- 1 ½ Teaspoon Ground Cinnamon

Directions:

1. Start by combining all of your ingredient in your oven uncovered for one and a half to two hours. They should thicken, and you'll need to stir occasionally. As it thickens, you'll have to stir more often.
2. Remove from heat, skimming off the foam. Ladle into jars, and try to remove air bubbles.
3. Can in a boiling water canner before packaging your jars.

Cranberry Honey Butter

This is another recipe that will go great with your pound cake if you don't want cinnamon honey butter. Cranberries are a fruity and seasonal fruit to give this butter a Christmas feel.

Yields: 1 ½ Cups

Time: 15 Minutes

Ingredients:

- 1 Cup Butter, Softened
- 2 Teaspoon Orange Peel, Grated
- 1/8 Teaspoon Sea Salt, Fine
- ¼ Cup Honey, Raw
- 1/3 Cup Dried Cranberries, Chopped Fine

Directions:

1. Beat all ingredients together in a bowl until blended.
2. Keep in the refrigerator, and it'll last up to two weeks.

Spiced Gingerbread Jelly

Gingerbread is a common flavoring for the holiday season, and this jelly is perfect for a Christmas gift. You can even make some plain cornbread muffins to put it on or a fresh loaf of bread.

Time: 25 Minutes

Yields: 5 Half Pints

Ingredients:

- 2 Teaspoons Butter
- 6 Ounces Fruit Pectin
- ½ Cup Apple Juice, Unsweetened
- 4 ½ Cps White Sugar
- 2 ½ Cups Water
- 18 Gingerbread Spice Tea Bags

Directions:

1. Bring your water to a boil in a saucepan before adding your tea bags, cover and let it steep for a half hour after removing it from heat.
2. Discard your tea bags, and then stir in your apple juice, butter and sugar. Bring it to a full boil using high heat, and make sure you stir frequently.
3. Stir in your pectin, and then boil it for one minute. Don't stop stirring, and then remove it from heat.
4. Skim off the foam, and ladle the mixture into five hot pint jars, leaving about a quarter inch of headspace. Wipe off the rim, and screw on your lids and bands.
5. Place in a canner, and can as directed.

Poultry Dry Rub

If you have that friends that loves barbequing or cooking, then a dry rub can be the answer. This gives a little bit of punch to poultry.

Yields: 1 ¾ Cups

Time: 10 Minutes

Ingredients:

- 1/3 Cup Paprika
- 1 Teaspoon Cayenne Pepper
- 1 Teaspoon Ground Black Pepper, Coarse
- 1 Teaspoon Ground Cumin
- ½ Cup Granulated Sugar
- 1/3 Cup Garlic Salt
- 1/3 Cup Sea Salt, Fine
- 1 Teaspoon Oregano, Dried
- 1/3 Cup Paprika

Directions:

1. Combine all ingredients in an airtight jar before gifting.

Cranberry & Pumpkin Bread

Sometimes a quick bread is the pick me up that people need, but that doesn't mean they want it pre-baked. This recipe gives you a great gift jar, and it's an easy bread for someone to make when they're ready for it.

Yields: 1 Jar

Time: 10 Minutes

Ingredients:

- ½ Cup Rolled Oats
- 1 Cup White Sugar
- ¾ Cup Cranberries, Dried
- ½ Teaspoon Sea Salt, Fine
- 1/3 Cup Light Brown Sugar, Packed
- ½ Teaspoon Baking Soda
- ½ Teaspoon Baking Powder
- 1 ½ Cups All Purpose Flour
- 1 ½ Teaspoons Pumpkin Pie Spice

Directions:

1. Layer everything together without mixing.

Instructions:

1. Heat your oven to 350, and then grease two medium loaf pans.
2. Combine all ingredients with a cup of canned pumpkin, ½ cup vegetable oil and 2 medium eggs. Stir until blended, and then blend everything together. Divide into two loaf pans, and bake for forty to fifty minutes.

Spiced Gingerbread Syrup

This is another winter gift that will help to perk up the holiday season, and it goes great with a homemade pancake mix or you can give it on your own!

Yields: 2 Cups

Time: 1 Hour

Ingredients:

- 2 Cinnamon Sticks (3 Inches), Broken into Pieces
- 16 Whole Cloves
- 3 Tablespoons Fresh Ginger Root, Chopped Coarsely
- 1 Teaspoon Whole Peppercorn
- 1 Teaspoon Whole Allspice
- 2 Cups Water
- 2 Cups Granulated Sugar
- 2 Tablespoons Honey, Raw
- 1 Teaspoon Ground Nutmeg

Directions:

1. Place your cloves, ginger root, allspice, peppercorns, and cinnamon into a cheesecloth and tie the cheesecloth together.
2. Take a saucepan and combine your water, sugar, nutmeg, and honey along with your spice bag. Bring it to a boil, and then reduce your heat and let it simmer uncovered for thirty to forty-five minutes. It should reach its desired consistency.
3. Remove your saucepan from heat, and let it cool to room temperature.
4. Discard your spice bag, and then place in airtight containers. It will need to stay refrigerated, and it's only good for one month.

Jarred Cinnamon Pancakes

Pancakes can be easy to make, but this jar recipe goes great if you're giving a syrup as well.

Yields: 1 Jar

Time: 10 Minutes

Ingredients:

- 4 Teaspoons Ground Cinnamon
- 2 ½ Tablespoons White Sugar
- 2 Tablespoons Baking Powder
- 1 ¼ Teaspoons Sea Salt, Fine
- 3 Cups All Purpose Flour

Directions:

1. Combine all of your ingredients, layering them.

Instructions:

- To make batter, combine 2 tablespoons vegetable oil, one egg, and ¾ cup milk to one and 1/3 cup of your dry mix. Bake like you would normal pancakes.

Blondie Toffee Bars

These delicious cookies are easy to make, and this homemade mix looks great in a jar too!

Yields: 1 Quart

Time: 10 Minutes

Ingredients:

- 1 Cup Flour
- ¼ Teaspoon Sea Salt, Fine
- 1 Teaspoon Baking Powder
- 1 Cup Light Brown Sugar
- ½ Cup Mini Chocolate Chips
- ½ Cup Heath Chips
- ¾ Cup Rice Crisp Cereal

Directions:

1. Layer everything together with the flour on the bottom.

Instructions:

1. Heat your oven to 350, and then grease an eight by eight pan. Add in ¼ cup softened butter, 2 lightly beaten eggs, and one teaspoon vanilla extract until fluffy, adding in your entire jar mix. Pour into the pan, and bake for twenty-five to thirty minutes.
2. Let cool before slicing into 16 bars.

Ranch Dip Mix

If you're looking to give a small gift to someone you care for that loves a movie night event, then ranch dip may be the best thing for them.

Ingredients:

- 1 Teaspoon Sea Salt, Fine
- 4 Teaspoons Chives, Dried
- 4 Teaspoons Garlic Powder
- 4 Teaspoons Onion Powder
- 6 Teaspoons Dill, Dried
- 1/3 Cup Parsley

Directions:

1. Just mix everything together until completely blended.

Instructions:

1. Mix with one cup of sour cream.

Banana Pudding Snack Mix

If you know someone who loves banana pudding, then try this snack mix. It's the perfect quick gift for anyone on your list, and there's no baking required.

Ingredients:

- 8 Ounce Vanilla Wafers, Bite Size
- 8 Ounces Banana Chips
- 12 Ounces White Baking Chocolate

Directions:

1. Just mix in a jar and decorate to gift.

French Vanilla Cocoa Mix

Sometimes people prefer vanilla over mocha, and for those people here is another hot chocolate option.

Yields: 6 Jars

Time: 10 Minutes

Ingredients:

- 6 Cups Nonfat Dry Powdered Milk
- 2 Cups Powdered Sugar
- 8 Ounces French Vanilla Powdered Creamer
- 2 Cups Nesquick
- 6 Ounces Instant French Vanilla Pudding mix

Directions:

1. Mix and add marshmallows on top if desired. Spoon into your jars.

Instructions:

- Combine three tablespoons of mix to every one cup of hot water, stirring until dissolved.

Conclusion

Now you know everything you need to in order to make the country Christmas of your dreams. There's no reason that you should have to settle for second best. Pick out the dishes that you want, and try them out before Christmas to make sure you get one that everyone will love. Many of these recipes can double for Thanksgiving and New Years' meal too! There's no reason to settle when you have various country cooking choices to choose from, so build a menu that fits your taste buds.

Merry Christmas to you and yours from us and ours!

Carson and Kathy Wyatt & family

http://www.FunHappyLives.com

Made in the USA
San Bernardino, CA
09 November 2018